THE TESTAMENT OF MIKHA'EL

A Hebrew primer to the reconstitution of the judicial institutions in the Kingdom of Yahowah and its people of Isra'el.

Michael Arnwine, Jr.

Copyright

THE TESTAMENT OF MIKHA'EL
Copyright © 2023 by Michael Arnwine, Jr.

Published by TAWCarlisle Publishing,
6161 El Cajon Blvd. #327, San Diego, CA 92115

ISBN: 978-1-958356-25-8
Includes bibliographical references.

All Rights Reserved. The reproduction, transmission, or utilization of this work in whole or in part in any form by any electronic, mechanical or other means, now known or hereafter invented, including xerography, photocopying, and recording, or in any information storage or retrieval system, is forbidden without permission. Please contact thescribe25@gmail.com for permission.

Unless otherwise noted, Scripture quotations are taken from the King James Version ® THE HOLY BIBLE, KING JAMES VERSION ®, KJV® Copyright © 1973, 1978, 1984, 2011 by Biblica, Inc.™ Used by permission. All rights reserved worldwide.

Book cover image co-created by Michael Arnwine, Jr. in part with the OpenAI API. Upon generating and editing the image, the author takes ultimate responsibility for the content of this publication.

Print book interior design by Traces of Design
Printed in the United States of America

Contents

Copyright ....
Contents ....
Summarization ....
Preface ....
Dedication ....
Foreword ....
Introduction 1
א Foundation 6
ב House of Isra'el 15
ח Wisdoms 28
    Returning To the Faith 35
    Rich and Poor 38
The Law 43
    The Law of Sacrifice and the Oblation Ceased by His Blood .. 49
    What of the dietary laws? 54
    Do Not Call Unclean What I Have Made Clean 56
    Let No Man Judge You In Meat Or Drink 58
    Punishment For Not Keeping Dietary Laws 60
What The Bible Says About Eating Pork (Swine, Pig) 63
    Unclean And Clean Foods 64
    Land Animals 64
    What Does Chew the Cud mean? 65

- Water Animals 70
- Winged Animals/Creatures 71
- Insects & Flying Insects 72
- Touching Clean & Unclean Animals/Insects or Dead Bodies 73

The Language 75
- God Giving the language to Abraham 79

The People 88
- The Enemy Within 88
- Personality 89
- Seeing is Believing 90
- Marriage 94
- State of Confusion 96
- Prayer 104
- The Aaronic Blessing 106
- The Sabbath 107
- Shabbat Times and Seasons 109
- Song Sung On Shabbat 110
- The Appoint Feast Days 111

ת Final Thoughts 117
- Christina's Thoughts to You: 117
- Michael's Final Thoughts 122

Torah Passages 128

Works Cited 132

Summarization

Michael's study of scripture in this book, and use of Hebrew, is a true primer for readers undertaking a journey to understand more about the bible. Michael so eloquently crafted complex details from his own 25-year journey to know the truth. He uses his unique perspective on Hebrew laws, and how they were fulfilled by Jesus. This book will challenge your own ideas with allegories and illustrations – by redressing misquoted biblical additives in a persuasive way, from comments on the lost tribes of Israel, the responsibility of Christians to challenge misconceptions on the proper interpretations and applicability of God's laws, commandments and statues today. Using the Hebrew language and diction, Michael will guide readers on the deeply, thoughtful plan of God and its mysteries for their lives.

Get ready for a steady retort of litanies and formulations from the Hebrew language perspective. It will certainly help you learn new insight into the Bible that you have never heard or explained before.

Preface

This book is to provide direction to any persons who want to know more about the God of the bible. It is especially directed to the children of God and is a guide to their return to the Hebrew language, to its people, and to the land of יְהֹוָה (transl.: "Yəhōwāh" or "Yahowah"). It is my hope that readers find this book informative, elevating their understanding on the mysteries in the bible. I hope you use this book as an applicable primer and guide on how to follow God's laws. It's my hope this book edifies God's people by bringing awareness, and insight to the priesthood, within the kingdom of Isra'el and the reinstatement of His judges for the remission of sin. As the Lord lives, I believe the most significant parts of this book are the notional views about the revelation of the diaspora's return to the judicial governances, times, seasons, language, and applicable practices of the laws of God. That by His Spirit, His people will yield boldly, their strength, in perfected joy and faith, without forced compulsion to do the laws, statutes, Shabbats, and Appointed Feast Days of the Most High God. (Exodus 18:17-23 and Joel 2)

Dedication

To my children (Heb. יְלָדַי, transl. "yᵊlāḏay"): Abigail (Heb. אֲבְנִיל, transl. "avəga'əl"), *your father's joy*, found in 1 Samuel 2-42 in Torah, and Hannah (Heb. חַנָּה, transl. "khanah"), *for the lord has granted me grace and forgiven my sins*, found in 1 Samuel 1:2-28 and 1 Samuel 2:1-2, and Ethan (Heb. אֵיתָן, transl. "êṯān") *for the Lord has given me enduring strength, to become judge and fore-bearer of sinners aiding them to overcome lawlessness*, found in Psalms 89 written by Ethan and 1 Kings 4:31. Here is their names together: *For the Law of Yahowah became my chief joy, and with His unfathomable grace He increased my faith with enduring strength to guide His people into the royal priesthood of Isra'el that will bring judgement to the nations for the remission of sin.* (Micah 4:3, Isaiah 2:4). And to my darling, wife, Christina, my chief advisor, friend, and faithful companion; may these words edify my love for you and sanctify you and the family to continually seek the Lord forever.

To the family and convert (Heb. מִשְׁפָּחָה, transl. "mish'pakha"): I wrote this book as a guide to you and to many families. May these words edify you and reprove you as choice silver. May it provide practical guidance encouraging you to keep the faith. May it help you remember your heavenly father's wisdom to guide your children's children in the Laws of יְהֹוָה (transl.: "Yəhōwāh" or "Yahowah"). Remember the summation of the law by the Elect One to "Love Elohim, His Words, His People, the land and convert, as you love yourself" (Luke 10:27-35) Remember you are royalty and the orientation of the Proverbs of Solomon's are for you: "It is to the glory of God to conceal a matter: and the honor of Kings to search it out" (Proverbs 25:2).

Foreword

We are going to do everything God called us to do in this family, in this world, to help people come to know Yeshua (who is also called Jesus) the savior of the world. It will take writing books, plays, music – everything and anything that is in us, and God will prosper our family and keep us. My grandchildren, they will be the ones who will take it to a generation that has never heard how great our God is.

Pastor Michael Arnwine, Prevailing Word Christian Center, Lancaster, CA.

Introduction

In late August, my closest friends and I typically meet for our yearly vacation. It's mostly an under-planned recharge and escape zone from normalcy used to reflect on the success and failures of the past year. Of course, being supremely under-planned means, it mostly leaves us wondering why we even subject ourselves to it, but it never fails to keep our friendship close. Sarcastically, our 2022 vacate was no different in that most of it was about a full-on competitive nightmare of events. Sam, the designated planner in our group, usually includes grouped activities to initiate conversation and engagement. Imagine for a moment being in a fast-paced, brain teaser, locked behind a closed door, trying to escape a fictitious criminal activity with which you are apparent. Can you imagine 40 plus year-old, 210 pound-plus, 6-foot, former collegiate athletes in a tiny room trying to pontificate the meaning of life while performing overly, confusing puzzles. The banter was just as bad. From miscommunication and 'mansplaining' that caused all sorts of verbal disagreements and afterwards. Our normal jousting, in fun lead to who performed better in locksmithing, puzzle mastery and the most useful person in the room. By the way fellas, it was me, write your own book (Laughing). And of course, it overflowed into every other event, from our favorite social electronic games to which movie was better. Most of the

Introduction

time our activities ended in exasperation from the whole experience, but this year I really needed wisdom and guidance for the next year.

You see, our time is during one of the feast days of the Lord, and being the only person in the room with knowledge of that fact meant I was seeking answers for myself. For the past two years, my wife and I had been aggressively combating stage-two colon cancer and after several non-invasive, unconventional procedures, we just got news that their delivery on promises were not as effective as we'd hoped. Her family history meant undertaking several arduous processes, and both of our stress levels were leading to disagreeable outcomes. I was under considerable discomfort and the stress was turning overwhelming and hopeless. So, getting away from it all helped me seek the Lord, through prayer and the special time with God, and made my desperation and sorrow dissolve into esoteric peace.

About three days into the brotherhood weekend, my myopic state began to clear. I remember this overwhelming need to minister. I started by asking my friends several imposing questions on the root of faith and what their desires were for a better year. We opened several discussions on the topics of discourse, fellowship, family, marriage, and the encouragement that lead us to address our hopes, fears, and future plans. When it was my turn, which meant I was last, my first thoughts innately were on my wife's healing. Lamenting, I wanted comfort on how all the things we tried, failed. I wanted to know how this would bring about her deliverance. I explained my faith in God, was assured we were not idle about all the medical places we visited, and how I wanted to know that Christina's joyful season would come soon. Not soon after, I added something that at the time seemed suspiciously selfish. I asked the Lord if He so found favor with me, that in the coming year He might appoint me to lead His people again. I don't even know why I made this statement. In the Spirit, maybe, I was asking for a new year of blessings for more work. Really!

Of course, my past experiences of ministry impacted my thoughts especially now after several less inspiring leadership positions. I was remembering a time, during my own days of hypocrisy, I unknowingly keep challenging leaders about *doing* the truth in the bible. Some unspecified Saturday morning, I remember one of the elders of our old ministry hosted a cleanup day at a church facility called Canaan Land Ranch. As normal, we used this time to promote and encourage the men with a teaching, but also expected them to take on the responsibility to clean up the ranch thereafter. Now about this time I was a budding religious 'practicer' of a newly formed idea called Shabbat, and feeling emboldened I may have openly addressed my concerns about working on these days to one of the Elders. After studying for 3 years in Yeshiva school (Rabbinical Taught Hebrew) given by the same church, the tenants of the commandment led me to want to commit to the practices of Exodus 20. Expecting a dialog, I asked one of the Elder's, "Should the men be here working, if the Lord commanded us to rest on His holy day?" Expecting a homily response, surprisingly his word fell a bit short.

He didn't quote a verse or scripture repudiating my youthful curiosity. He didn't even mention the humiliation of my request; that maybe because Hebrew was still new, that we were all still learning to appreciate the importance of God's Laws. He simply

Introduction

stated, "Michael how else am I going to get the people here?" Shocked, I got in my car and left.

His statement was the exact indictment on the premise of God's church today. Rephrased, he was saying "The needs of ministry outweigh the needs of The Law and its people are responsible to do the will of the church." This statement truly fulfills the declaration made by Samuel confirming King Saul's disobedience to God's Laws.

> "And Samuel said, 'Hath the Lord as great delight in burnt offerings and sacrifices as in obeying the voice of the Lord? Behold, to obey is better than sacrifice, and to hearken than the fat of rams'." (1 Samuel 15:22).

Now, if you're feeling awkward, you may ask if the Church or the foundations built are useful; if they edify by the Law and teach that in doing all the practices outlined by Jesus, including the Laws of Moses, then why are they postulating as influencers and then perverting the keeping of God's laws? The root of apologetical paeanistic followers was set, and now it was perverting the message of hope, overshadowing Jesus' fundamental premise to obey the Law of God. The theorem of faith-based teaching is in Hellenistic and propagandistic theism teachings which removed Jesus' fundamental tenants of Christ-followers and diminishing *that* was leading to an underdeveloped Kingdom. America's church, its ecclesia, which in the original Greek means the 'assembly of Israel', too lost its root by becoming 'practicers' of traditions instead of obeying

God Laws – and I was messing with these tenants! What was I thinking?

We were entering into the age of "manifestation", and through alms rather than obedience to God, I misunderstood that new age promoted enslavement rather than holiness. The adversary used our jealousy for wealth and property, laundered in deception, to help pervert truth that holds fast to the temporary benefits of this world - hidden in the rights of organized religion. *Ah What?* So, we got tricked! Because knowing that the foundation of Christianity, and continuing hypocrisy endangered the common good and enslaved people; I had really no idea what God might do to deliver His people and the grafted in, or that the clues were in the disdain of my request. Should we do the word throughout the book? Or is it a good idea grounded on Grace only? Should we test the truth and become what Paul called us, the people of God - to use grace alone?

Now, that you are completely sidetracked, let me paraphrase my thoughts. If we are God's chosen instrument to bring about His glory, and we, knowingly or unknowingly follow traditions, then at some point, God is going to ask us to leave those things and become more. *What should we do?* Start becoming His word and become a member of His Kingdom so that at *some* point we might begin to ask; is it better to obey than to sacrifice?

So, I started *asking* leaders, instead of sacrificing, how about we obey, and when I did that, I was no longer asking to be led, I was asking to lead.

א Foundation

In the introduction, I expounded on my experiences with my wonderful church, and the awakening God allowed me to know (even before many of my brothers), on the simple notion of the Word; that the Law is Holy and good for the edification of the body. During prayer time on one of the Feast Days of God, I made a request to God, that He might use me to do His Will. God then, and overtime, posthumously raised up my faith, brought confirmation by way of my father-in-law (as Moses did for Jethro), and made mention of the peacefulness he noticed in me. God used him in a moment of discomfort to give me intentionality as a kind of guide, and that these painfully enigmatic phases would help me understand that my affliction was a momentary pain, revealing His purpose in my life.

"And it shall come to pass in that day, the LORD shall beat off from the channel of the river unto the stream of Mitrayrim, and ye shall be gathered one by one, O' ye children of Israel. And it shall come to pass in that day, the great trumpet shall be blown, and they shall come which were ready to perish in the land of Assyria, and the outcasts in the land of Mitrayrim, and shall worship the LORD in the holy mount at Jerusalem."(Isaiah 27:12-13)

The Testament of Mikha'el

Reinvigorated, I began studying every day, looking for the answers in God's plan for His people. Since I already had about 10 years of history in Hebraic understanding of the bible, I used this perspective to research the meanings of Isaiah and Ezra; to understand the 'ingathering' and 'regathering' of His people Isra'el. My prayer time intensified, I kept asking people to join me in fasting, thinking God was using this time to help heal my wife, but He was using it also to prepare me for this writing. So much so, that I had to excuse myself over and over because the Holy Spirit was strong.

I felt for the first time, a desperation for God's people, specifically for the ancient diaspora of Isra'el, and the priest of Isra'el that has been lost, or worse, forgotten for well over 2,000 years. I really didn't understand that asking God a question meant He would develop a deeper desire in me to participate in the plan of God directly. He led me to several scriptures, and this led to several more. I began studying ancient writings, documents, books, commentaries, and I even joined a Hebrew language group, all from this deep impression that the people, the land of Isra'el, and God's words would one day unite in the Kingdom of God.

The story of my friends in the introduction wasn't about some deep meaning or to establish a philosophy. Instead, it was on the unique process God may use to keep you in perfect peace, and how he will use any moment to increase your faith. That doing the *word* of God, even when you may misunderstand it, is far better than sending gift or alms to an assembly or church. That asking for forgiveness of negligence to the Law is not Godly.

Foundation

Let me help you know this truth. If the world, being full of evil countenance, understands that ignorance of the Law does not subside (or lessen) the punishment therein, how much more demanding is the Law of God? It is my hope that many people who are blind to the truth will leave the place of hearing only, and become doers of the Law of God. Also, that through my journeys you may find greater fulfillment and commitment in what the God of the bible desires for you.

"All Scripture is God-breathed and is useful for teaching, rebuking, correcting, and training in righteousness. So that the servant of God may be thoroughly equipped for every good work."
(2 Tim 3:16,17)

To establish foundational premises regardless of the interpretation found in this book, the truth is, the bible was written by God-inspired authors, and is useful for the application and edification of the body of Christ. Throughout this book I use words interchangeably between English and the Hebrew translations, such as Jesus from the Greek and Yahoshua in Hebrew. If this is clear enough, explore with me our first notional idea that will be beneficial for learning and doing God's Laws. Since I am unaware of your background, I may unknowingly assume that you know a few guiding tenants from the word of God. So, to minimize the impact of any assumptions, let's establish His authority as supreme over all other gods. This book is adequate for those searching for truth, and I am confident it will help ground and reaffirm your journey. If you are coming from a Christian or Hebraic background, like I did,

The Testament of Mikha'el

rest assured in your faith that this book will certainly underscore your viewpoint and address several important questions.

In the matter of our foundation, I plan to pose and explain three questions.

- The first addresses the complexity of Jesus and how His life's message, and eventual death, culminated for the purpose of saving the House of Isra'el first and then the world.
- That the law of God is not done away with, and
- His people who are blind to truth must begin to understand they are the Holy people.

I use multiple references to describe how the bride of Christ will be revealed and glorified at the end of the age of the Gentiles, and finally, on the journey His people had to endure to return to the Laws of God to remove their suffering, becoming the firstborn among many peoples that are able to enter into the Hebrew of their faith.

"And we know that all things work together for good to them that love God, to them who are the called according to his purpose. For whom he did foreknow, he also did predestinate to be conformed to the image of his Son, that he might be the firstborn among many brethren. Moreover, whom he did predestinate, them he also called: and whom he called, them he also justified: and whom he justified, them he also glorified." (Romans 8:28-30)

Foundation

Here is part of the answer to a question about this generation, and what will become of the predestination ("where are they going?") and predetermination ("what is their purpose?") of His people. I am convinced His predestination is happening today, that even now, when so many people are deepening into all kinds of sinful practices, there is a growing, contrasting group, undergoing spiritual awareness. What is really fascinating is that these people are starting to ask really imposing questions, like what are the ancient days of the Lord? Is the current church of God adequate enough to equip us in our faith? I believe, yes, it is adequate, but it has missed a lot because of traditions. Many are using this moment, especially during the aftermath of the COVID-19 pandemic, to unite under a new banner called the Hebrew language. Further, many so called Colored Americans are asking questions about this new idea. Like, who are the people of Isra'el? Who are the righteous people of God? Can we find this correlation in scripture?

Now, if you heard this kind of message before, it would have been used to address God's plan of redemption through Jesus Christ only, but is there more to the plan of God? I think we have forgotten what the scriptures have reported about a group of people that are going to return at some point. Let us look at the following verse.

"... Hath God cast away his people? God forbid. For I also am an Israelite, of the seed of Abraham, [of] the tribe of Benjamin. God hath not cast away his people which he foreknew." (Romans 11:1-2)

The Testament of Mikha'el

For context's sake, this scripture is a part of a series of letters written to a Roman church, who at the time were a budding Gentile (meaning people outside of the Isra'el nation) assembly. Paul, the author of Romans 11, was addressing the concern or growing fear that those accepting the message of Jesus were beginning to believe that the Isra'elites in the bible, and locals, were of little to no effect. And Paul, being and Isra'elite, wanted to make it very clear that God's plan for Isra'el did not change, but was being used to help the Gentiles come to know Jesus. Truthfully, Paul's estimation was that the ancient people of Isra'el are not to be cast away but are in fact part of God's plan; their blindness would allow all nation's outside of the House of Isra'el to become the grafted branch onto the natural branch and called Isra'el or formally Jacob.

How did Paul know that even back then the Christians would at some point start to reject the Isra'elite people and this would lead to their increase in power; even overpowering God's people? Paul being a former member of the Pharisees, and being in strict adherence to the Mosaic law, understood the importance of God's plan for his people and was in no way suggesting we should abandon Jacob's people.

The people of Isra'el, or Jacob, based on Romans 11, were supposed to endure against His brother, and this continues all throughout the bible. Most specifically Esau, Jacob's brother, was both a victim and king. If you are unaware of the story of Jacob and Esau, it is an important story on the foundation of the two maternal twin brothers and nations that at the very birth were at war within their mother's womb. According to 2 Esdras 6:8,9, this is certainly possible.

Foundation

"And he said unto me, From Abraham unto Isaac, inasmuch as Jacob and Esau were born of him, for Jacob's hand, held the heel of Esau from the beginning. For Esau is the end of this world, and Jacob is the beginning of it that followeth."
(2 Esdras 6:8-9 RV1895)

This verse describes the power struggle of Esau, having dominated the world first, and that the beginning of the end of the His reign will be the beginning of Jacob's reign. Where now, it is so described that Esau would be present in this world along with Jacob. So, if Esau is here who are they? How does the bible describe Esau? If Jacob is identifiable, who are the people today? Could Esau, through confusion, pose as Jacob? Since Romans 11 speaks about their blindness, then anyone could pose as the people of the book. Is it possible that Jacob, who was renamed Isra'el, are the people blinded in part for all other nations sake? Does this new awaking happening amongst the people, mentioned in Roman 11, mean that the Holy people are returning to of the Kingdom of God? It just may be possible that the people who have been the most hated, without land or property are the very people God called His Holy nation.

I am not addressing this subject as an absolute, but only that you may consider the possibility that Paul's address would, at some point, wake up to the heritage of Isra'el. If God would not spare those grafted into the natural branch or grafted into Isra'el, who could boast against the blindness of His people?

As a Christian, Paul warned the growing national churches about such practice, and we know that the current people in the land of Israel have never experienced any boasting from

The Testament of Mikha'el

Christians. To this very day, the only group that is consistently marginalized, deprived of nationhood and land, language and identity by American Christian and it's leaders, are its former enslaved people.

Let's revisit a portion of this passage to understand the people:

> " ...but [rather] through their fall salvation [is come] unto the Gentiles, for to provoke them to jealousy. Now if the fall of them [be] the riches of the world, and the diminishing of them the riches of the Gentiles; how much more their fulness?"
> (Romans 11:11b-12)

The passage above speaks of a fallen time of the Isra'elites that would be used later to provoke Isra'el to jealousy, thereby having a desire to want the riches of the Gentiles or nations. See how its contrasting the same ideas that 2 Esdras proposed? That as Esau or Edom in the present age would prevail, Jacob or Isra'el would be as prey under all other nations; so leading to a collective jealousy? We know that the fall of the current Jews of Isra'el did not make any nations rich, but the fall of the enslaved people made all nations rich. If you are unaware that during the Transatlantic slave trade many people of Isra'el, with the destruction of Jerusalem, and after the occupation of the Roman Empire, and also slightly after the time of Jesus; many Isra'elites fled south to African nations. The Igbo tribe, for example, has been in Nigeria since the time of the fall of the King of Solomon and the 10 tribes of Isra'el went south.

Foundation

This is perplexing. How is it possible that the very people that are starting to ask the question of their origin are the disenfranchised enslaved people in American? Is it possible the Hebrew people in the bible this whole time were the byword, "Colored" people in America? I found an article in the Library of Congress in a Houston Newspaper that underscored this very possibility. Of course, I am not attempting to convince you that specific kinds of Americans may be Isra'elite, but that if they aren't, who would it be?

The Testament of Mikha'el

ב House of Isra'el

To establish the Word of God amongst His people, let's address a few specific undersigned meanings that were a part of slavery; (a) the adversary meant for the destruction of His people and (b) the explanation of "blindness" throughout the house of Isra'el as described earlier in Romans 11.

Romans 11 is speaking of a people that were under many offenses, were given into deceptions, and into wickedness because they spoke against the Most High and His Elect One. Let's also, take into account the historical record found in Mathew 27. This is when the people of Isra'el agreed to unify and put Yahoshua, or Jesus, to death. That with the chance to choose a more righteous path, the people instead agreed with the sentiments of the Rabbinical theocracy, the Roman government, and the Sanhedrin court to select a murderer named Barabbas over Jesus. Barabbas was a well known seditionist, Zionist, and murderer to both Isra'elites and the Roman people (See John 8:44, Rev 12:1-3, 7-9). He was used in the assurance of deception so that all wickedness in Isra'el was absolute in the following passage:

House of Isra'el

"When Pilate saw that he was accomplishing nothing, but that instead a riot was breaking out, he took water and washed his hands before the crowd. 'I am innocent of this man's blood,' he said. 'You bear the responsibility.' All the people answered, 'His blood be on us and on our children!' So, Pilate released Barabbas to them. But he had Jesus flogged and handed Him over to be crucified." (Mathew 27:24-26)

According to the end of the life of Jesus, nearly one thousand-nine hundred and nightly-one years ago (1991) years ago, the people of Isra'el added their own blood to be sacrificed and became a stumbling block. Who are the people who sinned against the Elect one (Heb. "Yahoshua," Eng. "Jesus")? Who are they today and how can we be clear they are the people?

Let's begin in Psalms 129, offering further explanation, or indication, of the people that were then called Isra'el. This parody used by my Hebrew language teacher may provide a clarifying contrast to the current people in Isra'el to how the proverbs of David described the Isra'elites in the bible.

שִׁיר הַמַּעֲלוֹת רַבַּת צְרָרוּנִי מִנְּעוּרַי יֹאמַר־נָא יִשְׂרָאֵל׃

רַבַּת צְרָרוּנִי מִנְּעוּרָי גַּם לֹא־יָכְלוּ לִי׃

עַל־גַּבִּי חָרְשׁוּ חֹרְשִׁים הֶאֱרִיכוּ למענותם

"Many a time have they afflicted me from my youth, may Isra'el now say: 'Many a time have they afflicted me from my youth: yet

The Testament of Mikha'el

they have not prevailed against me. The plowers plowed upon my back: they made long their furrows.'" (Psalms 129:1-3)

The referenced scripture in Psalms is part of a predication that repeats the prophesy of a prevailing affliction against the people of Isra'el. Notice the repeating phrase. This statement repeats to form a declaration or strong message that this will come to pass. This was also done to Peter (Heb. כֵּיפָא, transl. "keph," def. "hollow rock") when He was asked by Jesus three times to confess his love for Him and His people; when Ruth (Heb. רוּת, transl. "rut", def. "friendship"), the Moabites and wife of Boaz, great grandmother of David, cleaved to her mother-in-law, Naomi (Heb. נָעֳמִי, transl. "nā'ŏmî", def. "my delight") after being rejected three times, and her refusal to return to her own home land.

The Psalms prophecy describes how, within future times, the harshness of slavers from many adversaries of Isra'el, metaphorically written, will be epistles whipped as plowed lines in the backs of the Isra'elite people. This description is most notable because the current people in Isra'el have no recorded history of being whipped or even enslaved to the degree of "plowing furrows (long narrow trenches) onto their backs ." Yet, the former enslaved sent to many nations certainly have recorded history of furrows on their backs. If you are interested, search the web for former enslaved people with scars on their backs for a pictorial history. This is not written to the glorification of the enslaver or the degradation of the former enslaved, but only in the effort to point to the possibility that the Holy people of the book were in fact many of the former enslaved people. History is neither kind nor destructive, rather the facts, applied in truth, uncover this foreboding possibility.

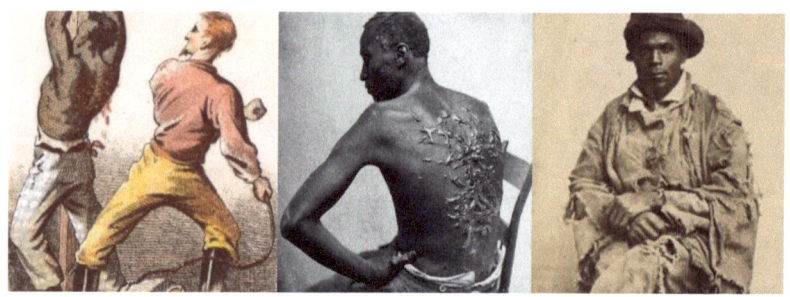

Let's continue. To further the investigation of whom might be the people of Isra'el, lets discuss the curses that would help identify Isra'el specifically and the impossibility and uncanny accuracy in Deuteronomy 28.

> "And the LORD shall bring thee into Egypt again with ships, by the way whereof I spake unto thee, Thou shalt see it no more again: and there ye shall be sold unto your enemies for bondmen and bondwomen, and no man shall buy you."
> (Deuteronomy 28:68)

The important point I want to highlight is the first stanza of the curse described by Moses. The curses against Isra'el would happen because God's people, at some point in time, would refuse to practice God's Laws. It's interesting that the last curse would lead to their enslavement. We will come back to that.

The Testament of Mikha'el

The people of Isra'el based on this verse would endure this curse, not by land with the hopes of returning to it by their own strength. Nor was it going to be possible to have a single leader born on land to easily bring them back in ships as one who would deliver His people, born of the Spirit. The liability would be upon Egypt (Heb. מִצְרַיִם , transl. "mitzrayim") again, the distinction is not that it would be done by land, but by ships.

Again, in recorded history the current known people who lay claim to being the House of Isra'el have never been sold into slavery nor set into ships. Yet, again, the former enslaved of America were sold to many nations during the Trans-Atlantic slave trade. Many were placed on ships, closer to 14.6 million people were transported with an average rate of 16.2% or 2.6 million dying along the middle passages.

Historians estimate that between 15-25% of the enslaved Africans bound for the Americas died aboard slave ships. Death rates, which were directly proportional to the length of the voyage, declined as the time of the voyage was reduced significantly between the beginning of the 16th century and the end of the 19th century. (Britannica)

The Testament of Mikha'el

The point here is we have the evidence of slave ships, and the current claimers of being the Holy people of Isra'el have never been enslaved *or* placed on slave ships. Even if they may claim they are the people from the original Egypt, their claims fall short, and they cannot maintain the claim of being transported in slave ships.

Let's break down the word Egypt, which is a bit different in Hebrew. The word "Egypt" is the Hebrew word מִצְרַיִם, transliterated as miṣrayim. The word Mitzra- means consumer goods in Modern Hebrew, and the work 'em' or 'im' at the end of a Hebrew word denotes plurality or more than one group or nation. In other words, "Egypt" is the statement attributed to multiple nations principally engaged in the capture and enslavement of a people through the use of ships. The first misrayim was named Kemet or "Black Land," and Moses or Moshe saved God's people by leading them through the great Exodus. The Exodus was by land and Moshe, the savior, was given power to free His people to establish the land of Isra'el. How much more will Yahowah lead the next diaspora from the land of their oppressors?

Which leads us to Moshe and his experience with the burning bush. One of the prevailing issues was if Moses was a black man, and also as a black man it would mean that the Isra'elites were in fact descendants of darker skin people. During the reading of the scriptures there was a concerning conversation between Moshe and Yahowah. Specifically at the burning bush miracle, Moshe was asked to perform several miracles:

House of Isra'el

"And the LORD said, 'furthermore unto him, Put now thine hand into thy bosom.' And he put his hand into his bosom: and when he took it out, behold, his hand was leprous as snow. And he said, 'Put thine hand into thy bosom again.' And he put his hand into his bosom again; and plucked it out of his bosom, and, behold, it was turned again as his [other] flesh. 'And it shall come to pass, if they will not believe thee, neither hearken to the voice of the first sign, that they will believe the voice of the latter sign.'"
(Exodus 4:6-8)

In the following passage, Moshe was specifically asked to put his hand close to his body so that it would be hidden. When the Lord told Moshe to remove his hand, his hand was noticeably white. I mention this only because it is an interesting fact that helps build the case of a darker-skinned people called Isra'el. God used the changing of skin color as noticeable sign for Pharaoh and his people to see, and free God's people. Another fact is during the time of Moshe's birth, Amenhotep II, who reigned in 1450 BC to 1425 BC, decreed that all male children be killed by throwing them into the river. Notice the similarities of treatment of the Transatlantic slave trade and how we were thrown overboard for various reasons. The story goes on in the bible to say that Moshe's mother, being unable to hide him any longer, appeared to obey the decree but instead put her son in an ark in hopes that he might be spared. What's important here is the daughter of Pharaoh, in the story, has compassion on this one Hebrew boy. Ironically, this princess risked her life by integrating a so called "white" child into an all-black family, effectively lying and calling him her son. If you are unaware,

The Testament of Mikha'el

Egypt is in Africa, and in ancient times there were darker-skinned people from the "Black Land." So, how is it that this baby can be hidden in plain sight with all of Egypt and be of a lighter-skin complexion? I propose to speak. For far too long we have undergone revisionist history that conquered and changed Moses' history so they could become Isra'el. This type of issue continues throughout history and is used to hide our true enemy, just as God hid Isra'el.

Also, let's review the word enemy, or foe, used to imply a past history or destructive past encounters. If a stranger strikes me, they don't become my enemy because the first action is only a redress to enquire as the nature of the relationship and will not warrant such a reaction. But if I am familiar with a person's cruelty then my reaction is guarded, and further engagements are met with extreme skepticism and aggression. Further, anyone would at some point seek to separate from any further altercations of errored history. This would be similar to the American historical record of errored interaction of police brutality and arbitrary lynchings, at the hands of color, black, or otherwise misinformed public. This was the first offense, where we learned of the brutality of slavery few endured. What then, will we in this day endure another? No, not in the same manner, for the Lord is awakening His people.

An alternative term for this moment is called the Great Awakening or 'woke'. Have you heard this word from the media? It's a relatively new term, but what it is meant to do is mock a specific segment of people's return to the biblical statues in both natural and spiritual laws. The returning promotes universal conformity of peoples to whom will expose hidden agendas, lies, and years of corruption. As the world could not perceive of Jesus as the Messiah, so the world or nations cannot perceive the truth or even conceive of the possibility that the people of the bible were the enslaved people in ancient Africa. His plan of redemption, and the end of His people's suffering, will end in the fulfillment of the time of the Gentiles or the end of Esau.

To continue, there is an additive plan, in a practical manner, called His predetermination. This is a fervent intentional timeline of the Lord's assurance that a people, before His return, would start to carefully observe His laws, learning His language, and assembling together at a minimum on appointed days so that this scripture would be fulfilled; "that He may redeem a bride without spot or wrinkle" found in Ephesians 5:27.

That a people would remember their former days, and seek to continually live righteously, shaming the adversary's plan to divide the people. That His Spirit would lead them back to a forward demonstration of fervent commitment to the commandments, laws, and statutes of the Lord.

The Testament of Mikha'el

Biblical Curses	Historical Records	Verses
Israel will be taken and sold into slavery and captivity	American Slavery https://www.history.com/topics/black-history/slavery	Deuteronomy 28:41, 49, 50, 68
Israel will have no power to stand against any whom stand against them	Roman Empire Occupation of Jerusalem https://www.britannica.com/place/Jerusalem/Roman-rule	Deuteronomy 28:25, 65
Israel will be sent to Mitzrayim (Egypt or other nations) again by ships and scattered among all the nations	Transatlantic Slave Trade https://www.britannica.com/topic/transatlantic-slave-trade	Deuteronomy 28:68, 25, 64
Exiled in the land of their enemies	Bruder, Edith, The Black Jews of Africa: History, Religion, Identity (New York, 2008; online edn, Oxford Academic, 1 Sept. 2008), https://doi.org/10.1093/acprof:oso/9780195333565.001.0001, accessed 25 Apr. 2023.	Deuteronomy 28:25
A very sick and diseased stricken people, at the bottom, societies with other races high above them.	U.S. Scientists' Role in the Eugenics Movement (1907–1939): A Contemporary Biologist's Perspective https://www.ncbi.nlm.nih.gov/pmc/articles/PMC2757926/	Deuteronomy 28:21-22, 25, 27, 36, 43, 59-61

Biblical Curses	Historical Records	Verses
Packed into Prisons and Jails	Slavery by Another Name: The Re Enslavement of Black Americans from the Civil War to World War II	Deuteronomy 28:48
An Unprosperous People	Unpaid Reparations for Enslavement — "Reparations advocates have suggested different figures for the appropriate amount of reparations payments. They estimated the value of wages denied to enslaved workers at $2.1 to $4.7 trillion in 1983, approximately $211 000 to $473 000 per Black individual in current dollars. While Craemer et al suggested figures as high as $300 million per person based on the value of lost freedom, wages, and assets, with compound interest." (Himmelstein)	Deuteronomy 28: 17-20, 23-24, 29-31, 33, 38-41, 44, 51

ח Wisdoms

Love the deeds of the ancient fathers, the patriarchs Avraham (Eng. "Abraham," Def. "Father of Nations"), Yitzhak (Eng. "Isaac," Def. "He Laughs"), and Yaakov (Eng. "Jacob," Def. "Heel Holder," renamed: "Isra'el"). Remember the deeds of your generational father (Heb. "אָב", transl. "ab," or "אַבָּא" "abba," Def. "Father is coming"), and direct descendant Mikha'el (Heb. "מִיכָאֵל", Eng. "Michael," Def. "who is like God"), the justified one, that returned to the ancient language, to the people, and to the land of Isra'el to become a judge of multitudes. (Ezra 8:8). Remember your grandfathers ("sabaim") Gilbert, "Papa," the kind and patient father; Michael Sr., "Papa Mike," the pastoral father who lost much but recovered all through the adoption of many sons, his faithfulness to God, and Milton, "Papu," the father and pillar of wisdom, and nin-saba ("great grandfather") Grand-Daddy Charles, the overcomer who struggled with sin by overcoming sinners.

In concert of the former, continue to love the deeds of the ancient matriarch's, Sarah and Leah, Ruth the Moabites, and Hadassah who was renamed Esther. Consider your ways by remembering all their love, teachings and faith. Remember your mother (modern Heb. "אִמָּא," transl. "imma," biblical-Heb. אֵם , transl. "em") Christina, who by faith followed her Lord, and lord,

The Testament of Mikha'el

overcoming the sentence of death with innumerable acts of faith through fasting, pray and doing the will of יְהוָה רֹפֵא ("Yahowah her healer"). Remember your savtotim ("grandmothers") Alice's determination to do the will of God, Ramona the teacher, student, and forbearer of sinners, Dorelle's hospitality to strangers which made many converts of Yeshua, and nin-savtotim ("great grandmothers") Meme-Ruth the 'Great' pillar of faith and prayer, and Mama-Irene the forbearer of sinners.

Remember how Belial, the serpent and adversary, set up his camp against the family's unity, through divorce, disagreements, disease and division. Remember the Lord's faithfulness unto a thousand generations to them that love him according to Exodus 20:6. "Whom by faith He stepped in and predestined us as overcomers of sinners through the spirit, His promise and restoration to repentance."

Remember how he helped us maintain our covenants, as we learned of the freely available gift of God in Yahoshua and that through troubles, He refines us as choice fine silver. That His teaching is to be at peace with God and His people.

The family is the center of His people's revelation and you must complete the journey of becoming judges found in (Heb. שֹׁפְטִים, transl. shōf-tîm) found in Judges 2:16, Exodus 18:17-23 and in the Hebraic names in Ezra 8:8. Meaning we must judge the nations for the sins and "deliver them out of the hand of those that spoiled them," (Judges 2:16). Study the ancient judges of Isra'el and how the nations were tested for faithfulness to the Lord. Study the book of Judges and become wiser. The Judges are leaders by their history and were used to help His people return to God. The twelve leaders who were judges of Isra'el were

Wisdom

Othniel, Ehud, Shamgar, Deborah, Gideon, Tola, Jair, Jephthah, Ibzan, Elon, Abdon, and Samson. Here is the mystery found in their names:

Othnial עָתְנִיאֵל ("Lion of God"), Ehud אֵהוּד ("united"), Shamgar שַׁמְגַּר (no translation), Deborah דְּבוֹרָה ("bee"), Gideon גִּדְעוֹן ("cut down or hew down"), Tola תּוֹלָע ("worm, which devours crops or plants"), Jair יָאִיר ("who He enlightens"), Jephthah יִפְתָּח ("who or what God sets free"), Ibzan אִבְצָן ("their whiteness"), Elon אֵילוֹן ("oak"), and Abdon עַבְדּוֹן ("servile, compel to labor") begat Samson שִׁמְשׁוֹן ("in or like the sun").

עָתְנִיאֵל אֵהוּד דְּבוֹרָה גִּדְעוֹן. וּתּוֹלָע אַח־יְהוָה מְאִירַת עֵינָיִם וְיִפְתָּח יִשְׂרָאֵל עַמּוֹ וּבֵין אִבְצָן תַּחַת הָאֵלָה וּבֵין הַשִּׁפְלָה עַבְדּוֹן שִׁמְשׁוֹן

> "Lion of God united bee, to cut down, and worm, to devours crops or plants, as the 22 Hebrew letters of creation of Yahowah enlightens who God sets free Isra'el his people from their whiteness ("a people under or of the oak") and from the humiliation of servility or compelled labor in the sun."
> (Psalms 19:8, Judges 5:31)

The interpretation of the names is about a people that use a culture of "whiteness" to enslave and compel to labor Isra'el. These same people would use this culture to agree with a destructive spirit over all other socially and economically

The Testament of Mikha'el

inferior groups and would be allowed to be shunned and spurned Isra'el.

The interpretation continues with the 'cutting down' of slavery, I believe began with the United States Civil War; and the devouring of wealth by 'worms' would be a sign of the end of servility or servitude of His people. So the freedom of Isra'el would come at the 'awakening' or revelation of Torah, enlightening their eyes, and by its truth, they would become free. The Lord, as He did with Moshe against the first Egyptians, delivering them by land and water, then from the enslavement of His people based on Deuteronomy 28:68 by ship, must end this enslavement by fire in concert with the return of Yahoshua found in Ezekiel 39.

"So do not fear terrors, nor arrows that come at day. Even when thousands may fall at your side, ten thousand close to you, none of these calamities will come near you. You will only observe with your eyes the punishment of the evil ones ("the wicked"). If you say, "יְהוָה" is my refuge," and you make the Most High your dwelling place, no harm will overtake you, no disaster will come near your homes. For he will command his angels (Heb. מַלְאָךְ, transl. "Mal'ahk") concerning you to guard you in all your ways." (Psalms 91:5-11).

Remember the Assembly, the Ecclesia of Isra'el is a place of refuge (Heb. "כֵּפִים", transl. "Kefim"), and a dwelling place where people can keep the faith, law, statues, and commandments of God (Jeremiah 4 and Mathew 16:18). You may at times become a forceful blocker to those who set their hearts on committing evil

Wisdom

against the Assembly of God. You must learn the disciplines required to be comfortable with uncomfortable situations, in that your direction is in immediate opposition of the adversary. Maintaining integrity and truth within the Assembly of God is charged to us at all times. This charge may at times set your house against leaders or man-made rulers. You must remain vigilant to promote truth to His people.

This is the meaning of Judges: Tell His people the truth of sin, love truth, and deliver souls from Sheol, or hell. Be in agreement with Yahoshua first, you must remove the bondages of sin, then you must be intentional to set the captives free from the yoke of false teachers who force compulsion over freedom. When you Judge a matter, weigh each against the law, the commands, and statues of God. You must never pervert justice (Job 8:3). Know there is no law against doing good (Galatian 5:22-23). You are a Judge of Isra'el, and you must love the faith, and never show partiality to the habitual sinner.

Maintain purity through obedience to Torah, which is your reasonable service, and become the holy (Heb. הַקֹּדֶשׁ, transl. "HaQodesh") people (Heb. עַם, transl. "am") again. Maintain the alms and keep the faith; carefully observing Shabbat and Appointed Feast Days of Yahowah. Love mankind, always apt to do and teach the laws and commandment of Yahowah, so that you may lay claim to the kingdom of God (Mathew 5:19). And when you pray, ask continually that your ways be pleasing before the Lord. Ask Him continually to remember His kindness to you and His people, to remember you in the day of His judgment and to remember His righteous ones and their children, that they do not perish in the way (Psalms 119:76, Psalms 2:12)

The Testament of Mikha'el

Remember our older brother Yahoshua (Heb. יְשׁוּעָה, transl. "Yahoshua," in Grk. "Jesus"), who is both Lion and Lamb. Remember to labor, becoming a lamb to the family (Heb. מִשְׁפָּחָה, transl. "mishpacha") and the convert, helping the people to keep the will of יְהוָה. Even in times when His people may forget to show faithfulness, or have lack of understanding, or are becoming deceived as Eve (Heb. חַוָּה, transl. "khauwah", Def. "life-giver") was deceived; remember they are Isra'el and the convert are one (Heb. אֶחָד, transl. "Echad") in Yahoshua defined in (Romans 11). As a people, they are a most holy nation, so you are to forgive them as King David forbear the sins of King Saul, blessed and reproved him in the cave, (1 Samuel 24). Remember also how Balaam, our enemy, was commanded to continually bless Isra'el; for his mouth was under the authority of יְהוָה (Numbers 22:12). So must your mouth be as a lamb to the Lord's people and remember when you fell, and were in need of His kindness to lift you from your troubles. Remember His people, may He raise you up to be Kings (Heb. מְלָכִים, transl. "Melakim") in the season of your procession as King David was raised in his proper season (2 Samuel 2:4).

Do not be afraid also to go untamed as the Lion on any that continually sin against יְהוָה or His people.

(Judges 15:16) These are the those who profess outward they love God, but deny His power, deny speaking His name, and refuse to do His Law (Heb. תּוֹרָה, transl. "Torah"). Beware of false teachers. They are known because they prefer slavery over freedom of His people through paganism, compulsion, celebration of false traditions or days, or practicing of qabal-lah (transl. "Kabal-lah" or "Kabalat", Def "earthly traditions") (Mathew 15:9). These are evidentiary in modern churches, synagogues and assemblies, because they profess the Lord is Yahowah Melech (Eng. "The Lord is King"), but their hearts are far from the Lord, because they are practicers of lawlessness and teach others to do the same (Mathew 7:21-29).

> "Not everyone that saith unto me, Lord, Lord, shall enter into the kingdom of heaven; but he that doeth the will of my Father which is in heaven. Many will say to me in that day, 'Lord, Lord, have we not prophesied in thy name? and in thy name have cast out devils? and in thy name done many wonderful works?' And then will I profess unto them, 'I never knew you: depart from me, ye that work iniquity.'" (Mathew 7:21-29)

> def: The word iniquity in the Greek means, "without the law or Torah, or contempt for Torah."

Rebuke them openly, because many seek a cause of rebellion against the Most High, His Elect One, and His people. Also, beware of various practicers of divinations, mysticism, idolatry, inviters of communication with spirits, cutting of the flesh, consuming blood, those seeking spiritualists, card or palm reading, or speaking with the dead. Remember the failure of King Saul, the satanist, who sought out witches and spoke to the dead, the one who killed 85 prophets of the Lord and how the Lord rebuked him through Samuel (1 Samuel 22:6-24:22, 1 Samuel 28:3-24). You must rebuke these kinds of people and their unrighteous acts of profanity so that it will not become death to you. I reprove you because I love you (Proverbs 24:16, Proverb 9:8, Mathew 15) — Jesus rebuking Qaballah or Kaballah, Revelations 3:19.

Returning To the Faith

"And will not God avenge his own elect, which cry day and night unto him, though he bears long with them? I tell you that he will avenge them speedily. Nevertheless, when the Son of man comes, shall he find faith on the earth?" (Luke 18:8 KJV)

Why is Yahoshua concerned about returning to the earth? After years of laying its foundations in faith, and at some point, in the future, this same faith is gone from within in His people. Can you conceive of a time when faithfulness to the ways of the Lord no longer exist? Is it possible that those who follow Jesus today have lost faith in the *ways* of Jesus?

"Not everyone who says to Me, 'Lord, Lord,' shall enter the kingdom of heaven, but he who does the will of My Father in heaven. Many will say to Me in that day, 'Lord, Lord, have we not prophesied in Your name, cast out demons in Your name, and done many wonders in Your name?' And then I will declare to them, 'I never knew you; depart from Me, you who practice iniquity,' (lawlessness)" Matthew 7:21-23 (NKJV)

Wisdom

So practicers of lawlessness or iniquity in the King James Bible are particularly important in that Yahoshua separates the faithful, the law abiders from the law breakers. What are those who follow religious beliefs, workings, customs or practices; and how would we know who are committed to doing the Torah or law? Returning to God is not finished in just believing in Jesus, but becoming practicers of His same faith.

> "You believe that there is one God. You do well. Even the demons believe--and tremble! But do you want to know, O foolish man, that faith without works is dead? Was not Abraham our father justified by works when he offered Isaac his son on the altar? Do you see that faith was working together with his works, and by works faith was made perfect? And the Scripture was fulfilled which says, 'Abraham believed God, and it was accounted to him for righteousness.' And he was called the friend of God."
> (James 2:19-23 (NKJV)

But what works? James speaks of works and the Lord rebuked works as a justification of knowing God. Then what of faith? And how can we attribute it to the glory of God in righteousness? How can we recognize faith when believing in Jesus is measured by specific acts of faith? Examine Abraham with me. That He the Lord, made Abraham as a demonstration of His faithfulness by a single act of faith. Through his faithfulness, he was given the rights of righteousness and called a friend of God. We are accounted unto righteousness not by works alone but in the act of returning to righteousness.

The Testament of Mikha'el

Righteousness is the return to the way, statues and judgments of Yahowah. Let me add another scripture from Psalms:

> "Blessed is he whose transgression is forgiven, whose sin is covered. Blessed [is] the man unto whom the LORD imputes not iniquity, and in whose spirit [there is] no guile." (Psalms 32:1,2)

Examine again Jesus' statement after his quarrel with the rich young ruler and exasperated arguments of the twelve disciples:

> "And they were astonished out of measure, saying among themselves, 'Who then can be saved?' And Jesus looking upon them saith, 'With men [it is] impossible, but not with God: for with God all things are possible.'" (Mark 10:26-27 KJV)

As you know, they did not understand that Yahoshua was about to die as God the Father promised for Adam's sin; that He would be the pathway to redemption for His people from this statement: Psalms 110:1-1 (KJV) [[A Psalm of David.]] "The LORD said unto my Lord, 'Sit thou at my right hand, until I make thine enemies thy footstool.'"

For the Lord will do it, be at peace, learn of His ways, do His ways, become the people of promise for the Lord will do it, and it will be marvelous in your sight.

Wisdom

Rich and Poor

וְיִכָּנְעוּ עַמִּי אֲשֶׁר נִקְרָא־שְׁמִי עֲלֵיהֶם וְיִתְפַּלְלוּ וִיבַקְשׁוּ פָנַי וְיָשֻׁבוּ מִדַּרְכֵיהֶם הָרָעִים וַאֲנִי אֶשְׁמַע מִן־הַשָּׁמַיִם וְאֶסְלַח לְחַטָּאתָם וְאֶרְפָּא אֶת־אַרְצָם

"If my people who are called by my name will humble themselves and pray and seek my face and turn from their wicked way, then I will hear from heaven, forgive their sins, an heal their land."

(2 Chronicles 7:14)

Money is a medium or platform of exchange valued by its contributors, its military or nation's physical strength to manage inflationary principles. Of all mediums, money is reverent and best managed in the performance of acquiring assets or in exchange to provide income to your family. The most basic description of wealth and its accumulation can be attributed to the development of a local farm. If you are unaware, a farm's unique property supplies its owner with amenities and substance for living. Then, the owner supplies seed of various edible plants, the farmer can nourish the seeds to maturity – to its fruticose stage. If the farmer is prudent by planting excessively in favorable years, all the excess can be sold at public markets. Be a diligent farmer at all times, by managing the proper time to harvest. Understand that money exists to empower your ideas and bring to life new works of faith. It is important to properly value the ethical responsibility of managing wealth.

The perceived value is defined by the speed at which you can commoditize current and future work or value. As I began my

The Testament of Mikha'el

career, I did not understand the value of work. I traded it at its lowest means because I was trying to break into the market. As a young person, always realize that value is based on the buyer's perception of the value, and imitation requires subjugation as a trade for learning the skill of labor. Regardless of the fact that you may or may not have known a subject matter at which you're attempting to get employment. In just one year on the job your effectiveness must be directly attributed to your willingness to learn from peers and superiors. I was able, through communication and friendship, to convince the employer that I could not only work under limited conditions, meaning low pay and long hours, that I was capable of leading others to do the same. I was so convincing in my first interview that the company promoted me to manager, which at the time I had no qualifications to perform.

It's important to note that qualifications are about perception, especially when the interviewers may possess less knowledge about the subject matter to determine your worth or value. I plan to discuss this more in the employment section of this book. Let's discuss the importance of money and why the accumulation of wealth is important enough to pursue. Money advances any cause of many subjects with only the cost of potential loss of the same. In the bible it says that money answers all things. Truly, money can advance any idea or destroy it with wisdom or lack thereof, to manage it. The trading of money to advance a business is about convincing a person or entity that you are capable of increasing their value and turning effort into more effort that leads to value. What a reasonable expectation. This is why most business loan officers will ask for your relevant experience on a new business idea before funding your new venture. Also, it is perceivable that the strength of a person's creativity and bravado are equivalent to the amount people that are willing to support or criticize the attempts of the relativeness of any advancement.

I had the opportunity to discuss the goals of increase with an associate one weekend till about 1 am. We began our discussion about the practicality of accumulation. He described his situation and used a word I had not heard in a long time -- Poor. His views on 'Poor' were about his perceived contribution to life in the value of his income. He would go on to say that he believed that he was poor because of the lack of discretionary income – by the way, this is income that can be used for personal desires. He told me the story about how he lived from day-to-day, working as a teacher and how he lost his job. How he was promoted to a director position and how inadequate he felt taking a position he felt he had not deserved. He went on to explain how at the same time of getting into a new position he was going through a divorce. His explained that his life just felt like he could not get things moving in the right direction. In his final orientation, he lost his job, family, and he felt like at this point, he was poor. I explained to him that that is not the definition of poor. Poor is a moral concept best left to the constructs of the morality protectors found in the wisdom of the Almighty.

What I told him from the ancient proverbs from King (Melech) David (Dawid), was he must intimately know both worlds from going between Shepard (the lowest work in Isra'el) to King (the riches in a nation). In David's prayers and supplications, he said, "Give me neither poverty nor riches, but give me only my daily bread." Meaning: If I am rich then I may be tempted to say who is the Lord; if I am too poor, I may break my covenant with God and steal. Both extremes lead astray even the greatest of us and we should constantly monitor our expectations and ground our personal desires with these moral compasses.

Over the centuries the concept of poor has been refined that even יְשׁוּעָה יְהוָה ("Yahoshua" or "Jesus") scoffed at Judas' notional attempt of defining rich or poor. Each day is a day of faith and will require you to consider God's purpose and your personal desires, and how they must coincide to the benefit of oneself and equally to mankind and the stranger.

The Law

What of the Law or Torah, and what should we do with it? Read Romans 6. My father's favorite orientation and paraphrase of this chapter begins with, "What shall we say then, shall we continue in sin that grace may abound?", and Paul unequivocally wrote "God forbid!" Even Yahoshua warned of those who would practice lawlessness in (Matthew 5:17-20) (KJV).

It states: "Think not that I am come to destroy the law, or the prophets: I am not come to destroy, but to fulfill. For verily I say unto you, Till heaven and earth pass, one jot ("yod", "'") or one tittle ("smallest Hebrew mark on a letter") shall in no wise pass from the law, till all be fulfilled. Whosoever therefore shall break one of these least commandments, and shall teach men so, he shall be called the least in the kingdom of heaven; but whosoever shall do and teach [them], the same shall be called great in the kingdom of heaven. For I say unto you, That except your righteousness shall exceed [the righteousness] of the scribes and Pharisees, ye shall in no case enter into the kingdom of heaven."

By returning to the ways of Yahowah, it is not out of compulsion but an act of faith and love. How deep is your love? Can you do it better?

Someone asked me once, should I do all the law? Is it possible to do all 613 laws? Can we be in Salvation and not do the law or better said, can the law be separate from our faith in Jesus? Can you become rich as the sweetest honeycomb? Can your love for

The Law

a woman or spouse grow deeper overtime? For surely it can, and yes you can, by faith, return to ways and statues of Yahowah. You can commit your ways to Yahowah and become Holy. If the people of Isra'el are Holy, then all the nations are Holy. For out of one act of faith, all become faithful, how much more the act of many that all will become Holy? How deep is your love for God, it must be deep enough that your trust in Him through obedience, is greater than your convinience. You can and you will be able to do the laws and appointed days of God. It begins with knowing who you serve and then by knowing more about His law or Torah.

וְעַתָּה יִשְׂרָאֵל מָה יְהוָה אֱלֹהֶיךָ שֹׁאֵל מֵעִמָּךְ כִּי אִם־לְיִרְאָה אֶת־יְהוָה אֱלֹהֶיךָ לָלֶכֶת בְּכָל־דְּרָכָיו וּלְאַהֲבָה אֹתוֹ וְלַעֲבֹד אֶת־יְהוָה אֱלֹהֶיךָ בְּכָל־לְבָבְךָ וּבְכָל־נַפְשֶׁךָ

לִשְׁמֹר אֶת־מִצְוֹת יְהוָה וְאֶת־חֻקֹּתָיו אֲשֶׁר אָנֹכִי מְצַוְּךָ הַיּוֹם לְטוֹב לָךְ

"And now, Israel, what doth the LORD thy God require of thee, but to fear the Word (the 22 Hebrew letters of creation) of the LORD thy God, to walk in all his ways, and to love him, and to serve the Word in the LORD thy God with all thy heart and with all thy soul,

To keep the Words in the commandments of the LORD, and his

The Testament of Mikha'el

Words in the statutes, which I command thee this day for thy good." (Deuteronomy 10:12-13)[*]

The words of God are life, and good for all Isra'el to keep, teach, and do. If this is true, what laws today are applicable? Are all 613 laws required and what *word* is so supreme in nature that all peoples must be subjected to it? This question posed to me by my sister-in-law, was one of the main reasons I wrote this book. I hope this provides answers to the fundamentals of godliness and holiness for applicable practice and teaching. If you read the passage above, recognize a form that is not in the original translation of the Bible. To establish a foundational principle, we must first understand the Word of God is good for the edification of people. That Yahoshua, or Jesus, *is* the Word, the Law, the Torah and the Messiah ("מָשִׁיחַ"). That through many declarations in the books of the Prophets and the clarification in the Testimonies of Mathew, Mark, Luke, John, the Testimony of Jesus in Revelations, and the specificity in the writings of Paul in Hebrews and Romans; the Messiah, who is Jesus, *is* the Word manifested and become a living soul. If you are Rabbinic, the characteristics of the Messiah are confusing in that the prophecies of the Machiach restoring the temple of David were not physical or in a building. And, to believe the Machiach raised Himself from the dead you would need to believe in the resurrection of the dead.

[**] The Word and the additional information in "the 22 Hebrew letter of creation" are changed to address the missing information from the KJV which is the אֶה in the Hebrew.

The Law

I would point you to the Shunammite woman and Yonah (Heb. יוֹנָה, Eng. "Jonah," def. "dove"). The first was when a Shunammite woman and her husband conceived and bore a son after they housed Elijah, (Heb.). At some point in the boy's early years, he dies from a head injury. The Shunammite, being full of faith, returned the body to Elijah, and Elijah raised the boy from the dead. Then, in the belly of a whale in the testimony of Yonah, Yonah dies in the whale and the Lord raises him up. If you can explain these mysteries or the possibility of resurrection, then you know it is possible for the resurrection of the dead.

Yahoshua also spoke of this saying, they being (the people that were asking for a sign of truth that He was Messiah), they would no longer receive signs and wonders but only the sign of Yonah. The entire book of Yonah is useful in the edification of Yahoshua, brings enlightenment to the resurrection and His majesty - described to be the fulfillment of the laws in Daniel and the destruction of the Temple. Even the salvation of the Gentiles is reminiscent of the Yonah account of preaching to the people of Nineveh and the Assyrian King's commandment that they repent for their sins against the Lord of Isra'el.

Then, what of the meaning of the restoration of the temple? Is it not so that Messiah was to restore the temple of David? Yes, but the mystery was Yahoshua, being the fulfillment of the Law, and the end of the separation of God and Isra'el, meant that the physical place of the Holy of Holies was no longer required. The restoration of His people Isra'el, and the stranger (Heb. גֵּר, transl. "ger") or gentile (Heb. גּוֹיִם, transl. "goyim," def. "other nations outside of the Hebrews") would mean all would be invited to the faith in Yahoshua or Jesus as the Messiah (Romans 2:10.).

The Testament of Mikha'el

Then, if the Law is useful unto Holiness, is it good for men to do and maintain to the same? In my office as judge concerning this matter and confirmed in multiple passages, both provided by Yahoshua and Paul, it is the affirmative; it is my conclusion that all the Law is good, performable and required. It is supremely important for those of the House of Isra'el to do and teach others to do the Torah of the Lord. This statement is a fulfillment of scriptures that the blinded in part will be unblinded at the fulfillment of Gentiles (Romans 11:25).

At the time of the Great Awakening, the veil of the sons and daughters of the Most High, whom were as perdition, stained with the guilt of sin against Yahowah, are now garments of honor.

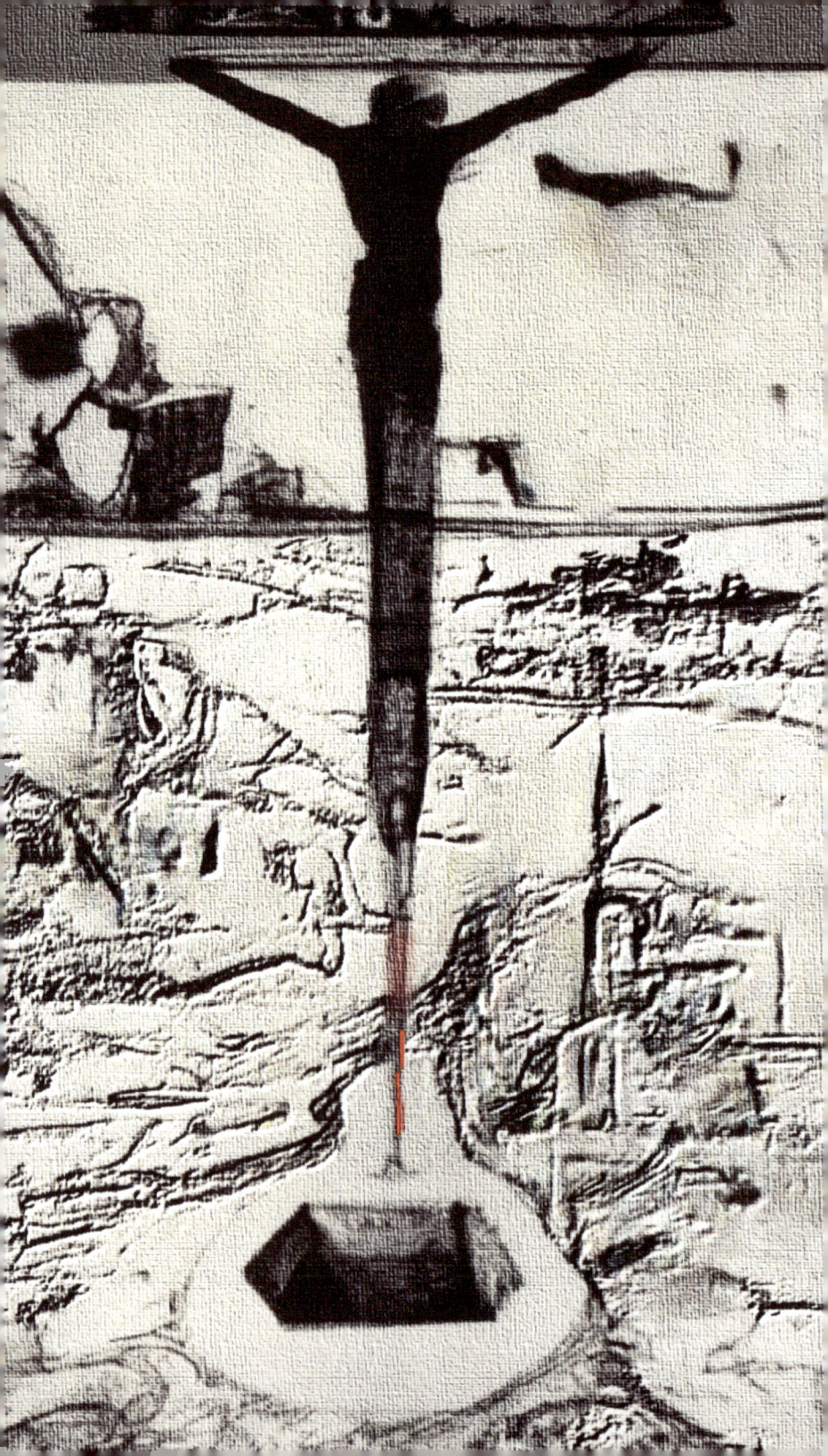

The Testament of Mikha'el

The Law of Sacrifice and the Oblation Ceased by His Blood

But is all the law required? No, not all the law is required but what specifically is not required and under what authority has this changed? You are correct only in the statement of the law of sacrifice and oblation; without Yahoshua we would be required, for the remission of sin and the removal of sickness and decay, to use the blood of an animal in both daily practice and in the celebration of His appointed feast days. All would be required to offer burnt offerings to the Lord and any feast as well that required the same. But Yahoshua through His blood, removed this practice as it was prophesied by the book of Daniel.

וְהִגְבִּיר בְּרִית לָרַבִּים שָׁבוּעַ אֶחָד וַחֲצִי הַשָּׁבוּעַ יַשְׁבִּית זֶבַח וּמִנְחָה וְעַל כְּנַף שִׁקּוּצִים מְשֹׁמֵם וְעַד־כָּלָה וְנֶחֱרָצָה תִּתַּךְ עַל־שֹׁמֵם: פ

"And he shall confirm the covenant with many for one week: and in the midst of the week he shall cause the sacrifice and the oblation to cease, and for the overspreading of abominations he shall make [it] desolate, even until the consummation, and that determined shall be poured upon the desolate."

(Daniel 9:27 KJV, WLC)

Again, to establish two witnesses, the book of Joel makes mention of the same:

The Law

הָכְרַת מִנְחָה וָנֶסֶךְ מִבֵּית יְהוָה אָבְלוּ הַכֹּהֲנִים מְשָׁרְתֵי יְהוָה

"The meat offering and the drink offering is cut off from the house of the LORD; the priests, the LORD'S ministers, mourn.

(Joel 1:9)

But how? You see, making something cease is not by statement or word alone; the Lord set this directly on the earth through Yahoshua's sacrifice where He covered all sacrificial requirements. If you are thinking like this, you are correct. Yahoshua (Grk. "Jesus"), to be called Messiah, was required to end the sacrificial requirement with His blood directly. In the verse above, it says the word, 'determined' in Daniel 9:27. That word in Hebrew means to cut or mutilate. You see Yahoshua was required to be cut and his blood and water was required to be poured upon the desolate. This was spoken about in Daniel 9:24, that Yahoshua would anoint the most Holy of Holies or desolate.

שָׁבֻעִים שִׁבְעִים נֶחְתַּךְ עַל־עַמְּךָ וְעַל־עִיר קָדְשֶׁךָ לְכַלֵּא הַפֶּשַׁע וּלַחְתֹּם חַטָּאוֹת וּלְכַפֵּר עָוֹן וּלְהָבִיא צֶדֶק עֹלָמִים וְלַחְתֹּם חָזוֹן וְנָבִיא וְלִמְשֹׁחַ קֹדֶשׁ קָדָשִׁים׃

"Seventy weeks are determined upon thy people and upon thy holy city, to finish the transgression, and to make an end of sins, and to make reconciliation for iniquity, and to bring in everlasting righteousness, and to seal up the vision and prophecy, and to anoint the Holy of Holies." (Daniel 9:24)

The Testament of Mikha'el

The word anoint in Hebrew provided by Strong's H4885 means to smear, anoint, or spread a liquid. What liquid would be smeared over the holy of holies? What is the Holy of Holies? This is repeated in Hebrew ("קֹדֶשׁ קָדָשִׁים") read verbatim, transl. Qodesh, Qadashim or Holy of Holies. It reads, in Ezekiel 43:12, and Ezekiel 48:12 as a witness to this intent.

זֹאת תּוֹרַת הַבָּיִת עַל־רֹאשׁ הָהָר כָּל־גְּבֻלוֹ סָבִיב סָבִיב קֹדֶשׁ קָדָשִׁים הִנֵּה־זֹאת תּוֹרַת הַבָּיִת׃

"This [is] the law of the house; Upon the top of the mountain the whole limit thereof round about [shall be] most holy. Behold, this [is] the law of the house." (Ezekiel 43:12)

These passages, in context, are consistent with the Levites oblation in both the responsibility to cover the altar with the blood of various animals and at the same time their portion of the land where the temple would be built as Holy. Is the Holy of Holies the ark? So, is it that the smearing of Yahoshua's blood would be required to be the perpetual sacrifice on an altar thereby directly ceasing the requirements of sacrifice and oblation?

"And all the elders of Isra'el came; and the Levites took up the ark.
And they brought up the ark, and the tabernacle of the congregation, and all the holy vessels that [were] in the tabernacle, these did the priests [and] the Levites bring up. Also king Solomon,

and all the congregation of Isra'el that were assembled unto him before the ark, sacrificed sheep and oxen, which could not be told nor numbered for multitude. And the priests brought in the ark of the covenant of the LORD unto his place, to the oracle of the house, into the most holy [place, even] under the wings of the cherubim." (2 Chronicles 5:4-7)

In Hebrew, the word most holy in 2 Chronicles 5:7, is ("אֶל־קֹדֶשׁ הַקֳּדָשִׁים"), meaning God's Holy of the Holies and so here the ark is described as the object of obligation of Levites to smear blood on the altar called the Holies of Holies.

Ok, so it is not established that the ark is considered the object in the prophesy of Daniel that would be required by Yahoshua to anoint or smear his blood on the most holy of holies. But how, wouldn't the ark be in the temple at the time of Jesus' death? Not according to Jeremiah 3:16 (KJV)

"And it shall come to pass, when ye be multiplied and increased in the land, in those days, saith the LORD, they shall say no more, The ark of the covenant of the LORD: neither shall it come to mind: neither shall they remember it; neither shall they visit [it]; neither shall [that] be done any more."

The people of *that* time of Yahoshua did not have the ark of the covenant and forgot its use, neither visited it. It was forgotten and buried in a place that Yahoshua would be required to anoint with blood and water. So, the ark was not in the temple at the time of Jesus, it was placed close to the Messiah to fulfill the law.

The Testament of Mikha'el

But why blood and water? Is it because of the scripture of cleansing a house of leprosy or plague (meaning to remove decay)? As it is written in Leviticus 14:51 (KJV) "And he shall take the cedar wood, and the hyssop, and the scarlet, and the living bird, and dip them in the blood of the slain bird, and in the running water, and sprinkle the house seven times."

To confirm this by two witnesses, it's also רֶמֶז (transl.: "remez," def.: "hint in reference to") in Ezekiel 36:26 "Then will I sprinkle clean water upon you, and ye shall be clean: from all your filthiness, and from all your idols, will I cleanse you."

But how would blood and water get on the ark if it's hidden in the earth? The account of Yahoshua's death may help bridge this understanding.

Matthew 27:51 (KJV). "And behold, the veil of the temple was rent in twain from the top to the bottom; and the earth did quake, and the rocks rent."

In summary, the prophesy and completion of Yahoshua's death, cleansed the people from all their filthiness. Remember during Yahoshua's death that the rock rent, for even the earth obeyed the Lord, as the disciples said, What manner of man is this that even the waves obey Him. So the earth split to allow his blood and water to pour on to the mercy seat of the ark of the covenant and it was claimed, tested and found by a man named Ron Wyatt.

Beside that point, this is not theory but had to be the requirement to fulfill this statement in Mathew 24:15, "When ye therefore shall see the abomination of desolation, spoken of by Daniel the prophet...", and that we are no longer required to split animals or sacrifice them for the cost of sin. In common reasoning and logical deduction, both Yahoshua's blood and water was required to cleanse the House of Isra'el by the Torah of Levities to remove the decay from the House. This liquid was an anointment and atonement to the altar or ark of the covenant known as the Holy of Holies and would have dripped upon the mercy seat, specifically seven times to cleanse the people of Isra'el and the nations for all times. It is thereby concluded and confirmed in the prophesy of Daniel, causing the Law of Sacrifice to be complete or fulfilled.

As it is written, "Sacrifice and offering thou didst not desire; mine ears hast thou opened: burnt offering and sin offering hast thou not required." Psalms 40:6, and again in Psalms 51:16-17, "For thou desirest not sacrifice; else would I give [it]: thou delights not in burnt offering. The sacrifices of God [are] a broken spirit: a broken and a contrite heart, O God, thou wilt not despise." Amen.

What of the dietary laws?

In Matthew 15:11, a commonly used scripture, is used to justify eating foods that are against Torah. The scripture is read in isolation; it appears the Bible is saying it doesn't matter what you eat, and it's what you say that makes you unclean, or a bad person.

Matthew 15:1-15 (KJV) "Then came to Jesus scribes and Pharisees, which were of Jerusalem, saying, Why do thy disciples

The Testament of Mikha'el

transgress the tradition of the elders? for they wash not their hands when they eat bread. But he answered and said unto them, Why do ye also transgress the commandment of God by your tradition? For God commanded, saying, Honour thy father and mother: and, He that curseth father or mother, let him die the death. But ye say, Whosoever shall say to [his] father or [his] mother, [It is] a gift, by whatsoever thou mightest be profited by me; And honour not his father or his mother, [he shall be free]. Thus have ye made the commandment of God of none effect by your tradition. [Ye] hypocrites, well did Esaias prophesy of you, saying, This people draweth nigh unto me with their mouth, and honoureth me with [their] lips; but their heart is far from me. But in vain they do worship me, teaching [for] doctrines the commandments of men. And he called the multitude, and said unto them, Hear, and understand: Not that which goeth into the mouth defileth a man; but that which cometh out of the mouth, this defileth a man. Then came his disciples, and said unto him, Knowest thou that the Pharisees were offended, after they heard this saying? But he answered and said, Every plant, which my heavenly Father hath not planted, shall be rooted up. Let them alone: they be blind leaders of the blind. And if the blind lead the blind, both shall fall into the ditch. Then answered Peter and said unto him, Declare unto us this parable."

Does this really mean we can eat anything? When read properly, verses 1 through 11, it sheds a different understanding specifically in Matthew 15:11. In verse 2 of the same chapter, the

Scribes and Pharisees are questioning Yahoshua about why His disciples specifically are not washing their hands like they do. Yahoshua replies, by telling the scribes and pharisees why they are transgressing the laws of the Most High. In particular, Yahoshua cites the commandment which says honor your father and mother. The scribes and pharisees at that time used traditions called "Qabalah"), that compels postulates to buy gifts for parents for a blessing to them. Yahoshua challenged them, by saying their tradition transgressed the law of the Most High. So, verse 11, refers to the washing of hands which the scribes and pharisees accused His disciples of not doing.

So, Yahoshua says it's not what goes into your mouth that makes you unclean, (referring to washing your hands before eating), but it's what comes out of the mouth that makes you unclean. The point is that there is no reference being made here to a dietary law, just the washing of hands before eating food.

Do Not Call Unclean What I Have Made Clean

Do not call unclean which I have made clean. This is another popular verse used to justify the eating of any food. When we read Acts Chapter 10 fully, which is where this phrase is found, we find a strong context. Acts 10:15 (KJV) And the voice [spake] unto him again the second time, "What God hath cleansed, [that] call not thou common." Let's postulate in context to grasp the meaning in Acts 10:1-35.

In Acts 10:1-35, Cornelius, a devout and God-fearing man from Caesarea, receives a vision from an angel instructing him to send for Peter, who is staying in Joppa. Meanwhile, Peter also has a vision where he sees a sheet with various animals and

The Testament of Mikha'el

hears a voice telling him to eat. Peter initially refuses, but the voice tells him not to consider anything unclean that God has declared clean. While Peter ponders the meaning of the vision, Cornelius' messengers arrive and explain how Cornelius was divinely instructed to send for Peter. Peter accompanies them to Caesarea, where he finds Cornelius and a gathering of people. Peter declares that he now understands that God shows no favoritism, and anyone who fears God and does what is right is accepted by Him.

In verses 1-5, we see a man by the name of Cornelius, who is described as being a Roman soldier. This distinction is important (you will see why as you read on), because he is not a Hebrew or an Isra'elite. Cornelius is told by an angel (Acts 10:3) that his praises and charity have come up to the Most High. He is told to send for Simon Peter the Apostle, and Peter would give him instructions of what he needs to do. In short, Peter, an apostle of Yahoshua, has a vision where he sees unclean and clean animals. In the vision, Peter is extolled to eat (Acts 10:10-16). His responses to the voice in the dream is that he as a Hebrew, has never eaten anything unclean before, that it would violate Torah and under the law he refuses to eat any of the animals. Peter then wakes up from the vision in Acts 10:17. Peter knows that it is not lawful to eat clean foods mix with unclean foods. As he ponders upon this, later on in the day the Spirit tells him that men would come and ask for him, and that he should go with them (Acts 10:20). These are Cornelius's men in representation of uncleanliness.

When Peter meets Cornelius, he tells him that it is not lawful for an Isra'elite to associate with unclean or other nations. But that the Most High showed him directly, that he "should not call any man common or unclean" (Acts 10:28). The Lord, through Yahoshua, was able to now clean all people who were submitted to His words. That the vision of the unclean animals was metaphorically applied to help Peter apostolate other nations.

This gives us a greater understanding that lawlessness is not allowed. That the phrase, "Do not call unclean what I have made clean," refers to human beings, or gentile (Heb. Transl.: "Goyim") nations. This chapter is giving proof that the Most High judges all men, not just Isra'el (Acts 10:34-35). These scriptures are clearly not making references to food, but rather the instructions to Peter and Isra'el to allow nations to keep the laws of Moshe.

Let No Man Judge You In Meat Or Drink

The next scripture in the New Testament used to justify eating any food, is Colossians 2:16. Here the popular phrase is let no man judge you in meat or drink.

Colossians 2:8-16 (KJV) "Beware lest any man spoil you through philosophy and vain deceit, after the tradition of men, after the rudiments of the world, and not after Christ. For in him dwelleth all the fulness of the Godhead bodily. And ye are complete in him, which is the head of all principality and power: In whom also ye are circumcised with the circumcision made without hands, in putting off the body of the sins of the flesh by the circumcision of Christ: Buried with him in baptism, wherein also ye are risen with

The Testament of Mikha'el

[him] through the faith of the operation of God, who hath raised him from the dead. And you, being dead in your sins and the uncircumcision of your flesh, hath he quickened together with him, having forgiven you all trespasses; Blotting out the handwriting of ordinances that was against us, which was contrary to us, and took it out of the way, nailing it to his cross; [And] having spoiled principalities and powers, he made a shew of them openly, triumphing over them in it. Let no man therefore judge you in meat, or in drink, or in respect of an Moadim, or of the new moon, or of the sabbath [days]:"

When we read the scriptures, from Verse 8, we see that the topic here is Yahoshua's sacrifice.

We are told that his Sacrifice on the cross blotted out certain ordinances (Colossians 2:14). These are the ordinances of the sacrifice and offering (Daniel 9:27, Hebrews 10) that I wrote eloquently about at the book's beginning. This is why some people at the time refused to accept Yahoshua as the promised Messiah and failed to see this as a fulfillment of Yahoshua. They would say that people who observed the Feast days (like "Passover") and "New months" observances without offering sacrifices were breaking the law. When we read the whole of Colossians 2:16, it goes on to include "or in respect of Holy days (appointed days), or of the new months, or of the sabbaths."

If we read the scripture out of context, it appears that meat and drink are the subject matter. But studying closer, it only shows that the meat and drink is in reference to Holy Days, New Months celebrations and Sabbaths. An example of "meat" or oblation would be the keeping Holy days without bringing sacrifices or offerings, which was a "meat offering." An example of "drink" would be no longer presenting a drink offering in propitiation of sins.

So, you can see Colossians 2:16 is not making reference to specific foods within the dietary laws that should be eaten. It is only referencing meat and drink offerings, which were laws before Yahoshua's death and resurrection.

Punishment For Not Keeping Dietary Laws

The terrible truth is that we acquire the sicknesses of the Egyptians is Deuteronomy, when we erroneously preach that we may eat everything we desire because of Yahoshua's sacrifice. This is what the Bible says will happen if you eat things that aren't supposed to be eaten.

"For, behold, the Lord will come with fire, and with his chariots like a whirlwind, to render his anger with fury, and his rebuke with flames of fire. For by fire and by his sword will the Lord plead with all flesh: and the slain of the Lord shall be many. They that sanctify themselves, and purify themselves in the gardens behind one tree in the midst, eating swine's flesh, and the abomination, and the mouse, shall be consumed together, saith the Lord. For I know their works and their thoughts: it shall come, that

The Testament of Mikha'el

I will gather all nations and tongues; and they shall come, and see my glory." Isaiah 66:15-18

These scriptures are making reference to Yahoshua's second coming. That during this time He will cleanse the world with fire. The world was once cleansed with water, which can be seen in the Book of Genesis with Noah (Genesis 7:1-24). It's also important to notice that there is specific reference to the swine, which is pig today (Isaiah 66:17). Reference is also made to the abomination and the mouse being eaten too. All of this should be a warning to anybody that is taking the topic of eating unclean foods lightly. To those that say that this is Old Testament, it is clear that this prophecy has not been fulfilled. The world has never been cleansed with fire before so it's clear this has not happened yet. This scripture also agrees with Yahoshua's second coming in the Book of Revelation (Revelation 8:7).

"The first angel sounded, and there followed hail and fire mingled with blood, and they were cast upon the earth: and the third part of trees was burnt up, and all green grass was burnt up."
(Revelation 8:7)

It is also referenced that the world will be destroyed by fire in the book of Peter (2 Peter 3:3-7).

"Knowing this first, that there shall come in the last days, scoffers, walking after their own lusts, And saying, Where is the promise of His coming? For since the fathers fell asleep, all things continue as [they were] from the beginning of the creation. For this they are willingly ignorant of, that by the word of God the heavens were of old, and the earth standing out of the water and in the water: Whereby the world that then was, being overflowed with water, perished: But the heavens and the earth, which are now, by the same word are kept in store, reserved unto fire against the day of judgment and perdition of ungodly men. But, beloved, be not ignorant of this one thing, that one day [is] with the Lord as a thousand years, and a thousand years as one day. The Lord is not slack concerning his promise, as some men count slackness; but is long suffering to us-ward, not willing that any should perish, but that all should come to repentance." (2 Peter 3:3-9 KJV)

What The Bible Says About Eating Pork (Swine, Pig)

People will always question whether the Bible says that we should eat pork. This is because pork is eaten all around the world daily, as staple meat. It is without a doubt a meat source that is eaten with regularity worldwide. The Torah forbids eating swine, also known as Pork, Pig, Ham, or Gammon.

Unclean And Clean Foods

There are five categories of animals we are allowed to eat found in Leviticus 11 and Deuteronomy 14 called

Land Animals
Water Animals
Winged Animals/Creatures
Insects & Flying Insects
Touching Clean and Unclean Animals/Insects

Land Animals

"And the LORD spake unto Moses and to Aaron, saying unto them, 'Speak unto the children of Isra'el, saying, These [are] the beasts which ye shall eat among all the beasts that [are] on the earth. Whatsoever parteth the hoof, and is cloven-footed, [and] cheweth the cud, among the beasts, that shall ye eat. Nevertheless, these shall ye not eat of them that chew the cud, or of them that divide the hoof: [as] the camel, because he cheweth the cud, but divideth not the hoof; he [is] unclean unto you. And the coney, because he cheweth the cud, but divideth not the hoof; he [is] unclean unto you. And the hare, because he cheweth the cud, but divideth not the hoof; he [is] unclean unto you. And the swine, though he divide the hoof, and be cloven-footed, yet he cheweth

The Testament of Mikha'el

not the cud; he [is] unclean to you. Of their flesh shall ye not eat, and their carcass shall ye not touch; they [are] unclean to you.'"

(Leviticus 11:1-8 KJV)

For example, a Horse has a 'parted hoof,' but it is not "cloven footed." Cloven footed means that the hoof is split into two, which means it's also parted.

You can see an example of this below:

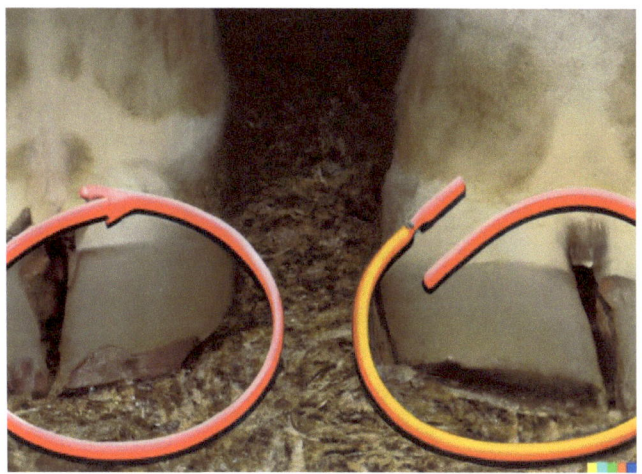

What Does Chew the Cud mean?

The biblical definition to "Chew the cud" means the animal is able to swallow food regurgitate (Cows and Sheep) or excrete it as droppings (Rabbits, Badgers). Then chew it again and swallow so it goes into the stomach, where the nutrients are broken down better for digestion. These animals are called ruminants or any of various hoofed, even-toed, usually horned mammals of the suborder Ruminantia, such as cattle, sheep, deer, antelopes, and giraffes, characteristically having a stomach divided into four compartments and chewing a cud that consists of plant food that is regurgitated when partially digested.

There is an exception though, we are not to eat rabbits, or animals with paws that can also do this.

You can see some paw examples below:

Keep in mind, the Bible definition of chewing the cud, is not the same as the modern definition.

To clarify, rabbits and some other animals have a process of chewing which allows them to further breakdown food. The difference is the food is broken down in their belly, and then excreted as digestible droppings, which they will then chew and digest. This is not exactly the same as rumination, which cows and goats use. The scriptures group all these types of digestive systems together as one. So, to eat land animals, they must part the hoof, have cloven feet and chew the cud. All three of these requirements must be present.

Chew the cud, but do not have divided hoofs.
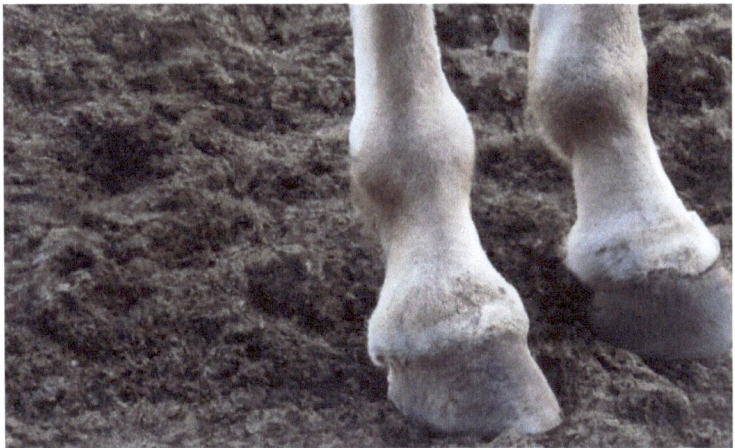
The Torah, as it is written, continues to point out particular animals that do not do this, so we are not to eat them. They are:

What the Bible Says about Eating Pork (Swine, Pig)

The Coney (which is a Badger)
chews the cud but it doesn't have divided hoofs.

The Hare chews the cud but it doesn't have a divided hoof.

The Testament of Mikha'el

The Swine which is a Pig (Ham, Gammon) has divided hoofs and a cloven feet but it doesn't chew the cud.

Water Animals

The scriptures for water animals, such as fish can be seen here:

These shall ye eat of all that are in the waters: whatsoever hath fins and scales in the waters, in the seas, and in the rivers, them shall ye eat. And all that have not fins and scales in the seas, and in the rivers, of all that move in the waters, and of any living thing which is in the waters, they shall be an abomination unto you: They shall be even an abomination unto you; ye shall not eat of their flesh, but ye shall have their carcasses in abomination. Whatsoever hath no fins nor scales in the waters, that shall be an abomination unto you. (Leviticus 11:9-12)

The Testament of Mikha'el

So, this is simple, if it has scales and fins, according to the Torah, it is appropriate to eat. This means, the seafood that people eat today are mostly unclean. Food such as Shrimp, Scallops, Lobster, Prawns, or Duck and more are an abomination to consume.

Winged Animals/Creatures

Next let's look at the animals with wings, and which ones we can eat. The scriptures for this are found in Leviticus 11:13-20.

"And these are they which ye shall have in abomination among the fowls; they shall not be eaten, they are an abomination: the eagle, and the ossifrage,, and the osprey, And the vulture, and the kite after his kind; Every raven after his kind; And the owl (Ostrich), and the night hawk, and the cuckow, and the hawk after his kind, And the little owl, and the cormorant, and the great owl, And the swan, and the pelican, and the gier eagle, And the stork, the heron after her kind, and the lapwing, and the bat. All fowls that creep, going upon *all* four, shall be an abomination unto you" (Leviticus 11:13-20)

With the Winged animals, the Most High, gives us a list of winged animal families that we cannot eat. Which means if a winged animal is not part of one of the families listed in Leviticus 11:13-20 it can be eaten. Keep in mind, these are winged animals, whether they can fly or not, doesn't matter. Each of the winged animals listed are from a family of other winged animals (birds), so if we find birds that are in the same family as the ones mentioned above, they are off limits too. The scriptures use the words "after his kind," meaning similar to. For example, a "Duck" and "Swan" are of the same kind etc.

Forbidden winged creatures we cannot eat:
    Eagle, Ossifrage, Osprey,
    Vulture, Kite after his kind;
    Raven
    Ostrich, Night hawk, Cuckow, and Hawks after his kind,
    The little owl, Cormorant, and Great owl,
    Swan, Pelican, and Gier eagle,
    Stork, the Heron after her kind,
    Lapwing, and the Bat.
Allow winged creatures or birds we can eat:
    Pigeon, Doves
    Chicken, Turkey, and Rooster

Just for notation sake, I would skip the pigeon as well, they are rats with wings in my opinion.

Insects & Flying Insects

The scriptures will show you the flying insects that we can eat:

"Yet these may ye eat of every flying creeping thing that goeth upon all four, which have legs above their feet, to leap withal upon the earth; Even these of them ye may eat; the locust after his kind,

and the bald locust after his kind, and the beetle after his kind, and the grasshopper after his kind. But all other flying creeping things, which have four feet, shall be an abomination unto you."
(Leviticus 11:21-23)

We're told that the majority of insects that have four feet and fly cannot be eaten. The exception are winged insects which have legs above their four legs that are used to make them leap far.

These include the following:
   Locust after his kind
   Bald Locust after his kin
   Beetle after his kind (Not a regular beetle that doesn't jump, and it must have wings)
   Grasshopper after his kind

Touching Clean & Unclean Animals/Insects or Dead Bodies

For the final part, we can look at a recurring commandment after each type of animal or creature that is unclean or clean to eat. This command tells us not to touch the carcass (dead body) of any of these insects or animals. Touching the carcass (dead body) makes us unclean until the evening. We are to wash our clothes and garments, but still remain unclean until the evening. The dietary laws give us a better understanding about the Most High. They show that the Most High really values the life of his creation, because there are penalties when we touch their dead

What the Bible Says about Eating Pork (Swine, Pig)

bodies. Being ceremonially unclean, results in an Isra'elite, or a convert from another nation not being able to keep an appointed day, such as Passover. So, remaining spiritually clean at all times is something that should make believers conscious of what they're doing from day to day. The next time you swat a fly or kill an ant with your hand, you should remember it makes you a temporary outcast (unclean until evening).

The Language

At the beginning, the Lord seeks to return His people to His way. In every way, He calls on them, but they cannot understand His words. How can His people, who are called by His name, not hear their Lord, Husband and King? Just as a spouse cannot be separated from a mate without a writ of divorce, so it is that the Lord cannot be separated from His people and His name. Just as יְשׁוּעָה ("Yahoshua" or "Jesus") is not able to separate himself from the language of his name, "Yah Saves," so we cannot separate from the language of our name Isra'el. So, I hope to expand your understanding; to deepen your commitment to the Lord; and pray with words emboldened by His people to return to the Biblical Hebrew language. You may ask how I know what the right path is. This is summed up in the statement, His ways are Higher than our ways, so His thoughts are higher than our thoughts. For the Lord knows the way of the righteous, and seeking wisdom and knowledge leads to understanding.

To begin, you must study to show yourself approved unto God. The fundamentals of the Hebrew language are the beginning. You must learn from the past to strongly grasp the mightiest of the future. See me as the past, that you may prove to be called sons and daughters of the living God; a holy people again.

The Language

The name of God is described by the Tetragrammaton ("YHWH") in Hebrew letters יהוה. Tetragrammaton means the four-letter Hebrew theorem or the study of the proper name of a deity. It's a bit technical, I know, but just hang with me. We know that His name is a strong tower and with His name we are able to move mountains and overcome suffering.

מִגְדַּל־עֹז שֵׁם יְהוָה בּוֹ־יָרוּץ צַדִּיק וְנִשְׂגָּב

Migedal-oz Shem Yahowah bo-yarus sadiq wenisegab

The name Yahowah [is a] strong tower: the just, righteous, lawful ones run into it, and are safe.

You may have heard Rabbinic teachers shun from saying the name of God. They believe His name is too Holy to speak and demonstrates impiety. Honor God's name as Holy, knowing this is the first commandment with a promise. We should not take the name of the Lord God in vain. That did not say to shun its very use. If that is true, then what should we do with the following scripture.

הוֹדוּ לַיהוָה קִרְאוּ בִשְׁמוֹ הוֹדִיעוּ בָעַמִּים עֲלִילֹתָיו

Hodu la Yahowah qireu bishemo hodiu ba'ammim aliylotayw

"Give thanks unto Yahowah, call upon His name, make known His deeds among the people."

(1 Chronicles 16:8)

The Testament of Mikha'el

Or this passage:

כִּי בִי חָשַׁק וַאֲפַלְּטֵהוּ אֲשַׂגְּבֵהוּ כִּי־יָדַע שְׁמִי׃
יִקְרָאֵנִי וְאֶעֱנֵהוּ עִמּוֹ־אָנֹכִי בְצָרָה אֲחַלְּצֵהוּ וַאֲכַבְּדֵהוּ

"Because he hath set his love upon me, therefore will I deliver him: I will set him on high, because he hath known my name. He shall call upon me, and I will answer him: I will be with him in trouble; I will deliver him, and honor him." (Psalm 91:14,15)

So, we must put the thought of "it's too Holy" to rest. Let's use a bit of circular logic. If the Lord, according to the commandments, said, "Do not take the Lord's name in vain," and according to Rabbinic Talmud, we are not even allowed to say His name aloud, then this commandment is overstated and redundant. The Lord knew His name would be spoken and used regularly in vocal arrangements all over the earth. His warnings and commandments were guidelines on the proper adjudication of His name.

In a few paragraphs, I'm going to teach you His name. But before that, we must establish how to read the Hebrew language so you can read His name properly. Hebrew is read from right to left, or from the stronger-vessel to the weaker-vessel, or from the traditional strong hand, which is the right hand, to the weaker left hand.

Before I establish this question, I want to expand your knowledge by showing a picture of the changes in Hebrew over the centuries.

English equivalent of the Hebrew "Tetragrammaton"'

Hebrew is written from right to left ←

The same "Tetragrammaton" in Paleo Hebrew,
-first recorded Hebrew Bible written

Masoretic-Hebrew adds vowel sounds (T) invented by Masoretes in 600 AD. Jesus would have spoken and read in Aramaic-Hebrew, meaning without vowels.

The Testament of Mikha'el

During my studies with Moreh Jediyah Melek, and the assembly ("עֵדָה"), he laid out how to properly read and sound the name of the Lord's Tetragrammaton. יהוה means, the Eternal One or "Who was, Who is, and Who will be." It's pronounced using the transliteration 'Yah-ho-wah' found in Genesis 3:14 in Hebrew.

Try it! Say, 'Yah-ho-wah'. If you feel a bit uncomfortable, that is normal. If you are a Christian or familiar with the word, Hallelujah, you may have unknowingly been saying his name for years. Let's fix the word slightly to address any "J's" in Hebrew. "J" does not exist in Hebrew. "J" is a "Y." So, it reads Hallelu-Yah or Praise Yah. Yah is the short form for Yahowah. If you know about the prophet Obadiah, written in Hebrew, it should be Obadi-Yah meaning the servant of Yahowah. So, let's try again, 'Yah-ho-wah'. You are to call upon His name, O righteous ones. Make His name, and His deeds known throughout the earth. (1Chronicals 16:8, and Psalms 105:1)

God Giving the language to Abraham

So, my question starts with reading scriptures, and continues with why would the Lord talk with His people in Hebrew? What is this saying? Why would the Lord cause an awakening to return to ancient understanding? Family, I want to explain this meaning to you so that it might inspire your curiosity to venture into the language as well. I want to draw your attention specifically to the patriarchs in the Bible. God purposefully taught them the language and a few nuances in the bible from numerology to describing the language disparities between current translations of the Bible.

The first and most well described historical record of the Hebrew language given, would be in the book of the Jubilees. In the Jubilees, Chapter 12, starting fromt verse 16-31 for context. It begins with Avram ("אַבְרָם") praying to God, to whom he did not know, extolling God as the creator of all things. In his exhortation he asked God to lead him to a new place where he could learn only of the Lord, and live in the way of יְהוָֹה. As the verses continue, יְהוָֹה blessed Avram, telling him he would become a great nation. He opened his ears and tongue to learn all the new sounds, and then He instructed the mal'ahk ("angles") to teach Avram a language that he might know the mysteries and seasons. Our patriarch Avraham("אַבְרָהָם") learned ancient Hebrew in 6 months. The Lord expanded his understanding and called it the tongue of creation.

The father of the faith, in his beginning, was given the language of Hebrew. Why did God desire for His people to know the language also? Why is it necessary for the fundamental understanding of His word, law, statues, and commands? I would focus on the *word* of God so that we would not be confused by the word. If I read it in the ancient text, no one would be able to confuse its meaning.

In my direct exploration of the word, the current translations like the King James Bible (and many others) provide, at best, a singular dimensional understanding. Here is my best revelation. The Hebrew language provides a multidimensional understanding, where a single word complexity means it may be multi-definitional and multiple numerations, and be prophetic

The Testament of Mikha'el

(to see into the future). Let me expound on this point by referencing a familiar verse in Genesis from my studies of biblical Hebrew.

בְּרֵאשִׁית בָּרָא אֱלֹהִים אֵת הַשָּׁמַיִם וְאֵת הָאָרֶץ:

Bereshit barah elohim et, hashamayim we'et haeres

In a beginning God created twenty-two hebraic letters, the heavens, and the earth. (Genesis 1:1) [Transliteration by M. Arnwine, Jr.]

The English translation does not translate the Aleph and the Tau ("אֵת"). The transliteration of ("אֵת") is missing. In studying with my teacher, the ("אֵת"), is the formation of words, or the shorthand for the aleph-bat similar to our Alphabet. Before the creation of ideas, a baby's birth and the creation of all things; words must be formed. You must agree by words then life will come. You must agree by words then hope will come. This continues throughout translations and as a result readers only know God in simplicity, but I am exposing the irresponsibility of the translators by correcting the knowledge of God by helping you see that it starts with words.

Let's take a look at another multidimensional example from a biblical Hebraic perspective. God, who inspired the names of Adam to Noah in Genesis, uses their names to describe his plan of redemption for Isra'el and the world. In the generations between Adam and Noah, a teacher helped outlined the Hebrew names and their meanings into a Hebrew and English sentence. Of course, her interpretation was not from a Biblical Hebrew perspective, so I rewrote it from Genesis 5.

The Language

Adam אָדָם ("Man"), begat Abel הֶבֶל ("Breath"), Abel begat Seth שִׁית ("Brings"), Seth begat Enosh אֱנוֹשׁ ("Mortal"), Enosh begat Kenan spelled Cain-an קָנָן ("Nestling like a Viper or Trap"), Kenan begat Mahalaleel מַהֲלַלְאֵל ("Praise Of God"), Mahalaleel begat Jared יֶרֶד ("Descent"), Jerad begat Enoch or Chanok חֲנוֹךְ ("Dedicate, teach, to train up"), Enoch begat Methushelah מְתוּשֶׁלַח ("Man put to death or dart or sword"), Methuselah begat Lemech לֶמֶךְ (no translation), and Lemech begat Noah נֹחַ ("Gives Rest and Comfort").

הָרִאישׁוֹן אָדָם הֶבֶל שִׁית אֱנוֹשׁ־אָדָם הַקֲנָנָה. וּמַהֲלַלְאֵל יֶרֶד חֲנוֹךְ לִמְתוּשֶׁלַח מִי נֹחַ.

The first Man's Breath Brings Mortal-man into a Nest or trap like a viper, but God Be Praised, a Descent-one will Train or Teach them, by a Man to be put to death, who Gives Rest and Comfort. [Transliterated by M. Arnwine, JR.]

To understand this mystery, refer to Hebrews 7:6-9, where it expounds on the mystery of the '*descent-one*' who would have no earthly-fathered birth. Who is the king of glory, the Lord Most High, Yahoshua. You must know His language, how it is formed, how it's sounds, then when reading His Word you can be introduced to new wisdoms and mysteries of God. As it is written by King David, "Surely I have behaved and quieted myself, as a child that is weaned of his mother: my soul is even as a weaned child." (Psalms 131:2); and Luke 18:17 states, "Verily I say unto you, whosoever shall not receive the kingdom

The Testament of Mikha'el

of God as a little child shall in no wise enter therein." You must submit or, better said, be agreeable, as children, to learn and be teachable, so that the latest information, latest ideas and new concepts can change unholy traditions.

To keep you thinking, I listed that names of God that you can use throughout your daily life.

God Is...

Hebrew	Transliteration	Definition	Reference
אֵל עֶלְיוֹן	El-Elyon	God Most High	Gen. 14:18-22
אֵל קַנָּא	El-Kanna	Jealous God	Exod. 34:14
אֵל עוֹלָם	El-Olam	Eternal God	Gen. 21:33
אֵל שַׁדַּי	El-Shaddai	God Almighty	Gen. 17:1
הַלְלוּ־יָהּ	Hallu-Yah	Praise Yah	Ps. 150:1
יְהֹוָה	Yahowah	YHWH	Gen 3:14, Exod. 6:2-3
יְהֹוָה אֲדוֹן כָּל־הָאָרֶץ	Yahowah-Adon Kal Ha'arets	Lord of All the Earth	Josh. 3:13
יְהֹוָה בָּרָא	Yahowah-Bara	Lord is Creator	Isa. 40:28
יְהֹוָה מָגֵן וַחֶרֶב	Yahowah-Magen Wa Chereb	Lord is Shield and Sword	Deut. 33:29
יְהֹוָה אֵלִי	Yahowah-Eli	Lord is My God	Ps. 18:2
יְהֹוָה אֱלֹהֵינוּ	Yahowah-Elohenu	Lord is Our God	Exod. 8:10
יְהֹוָה גִּבּוֹר מִלְחָמָה	Yahowah-Gibbor Al Milchamah	Lord is Mighty in Battle	Ps. 24:8
יְהֹוָה עִזּוּז וְגִבּוֹר	Yahowah-Izzuz Wa Gibor	Lord is Strong and Mighty	Ps. 24:8
יְהֹוָה מוֹשִׁיעֵךְ וְגֹאֲלֵךְ	Yahowah-Mo'shiyeka Wa Go'aleka	Lord Your Savior and Your Redeemer	Isa. 49:26, 60:16
הַמֶּלֶךְ יְהֹוָה	Ha'Melech Yahowah	The King Yah	Ps. 98:6
יְהֹוָה הַשֹּׁפֵט	Yahowah-Ha'Shofet	Lord is the Judge	Judg. 11:27
יְהֹוָה הוֹשִׁיעָה	Yahowah-Yahoshua	Lord The Savior	Ps. 20:9, Isa 26:1
יְהֹוָה יִרְאֶה	Yahowah-Yir'eh or Jireh	Lord Sees, the Way	Gen. 22:14
יְהֹוָה מָגֵן	Yahowah-Kabodhi	Lord My Glory	Ps. 3:3

The Testament of Mikha'el

יְהוָה קֶרֶן־יִשְׁעִי	Yahowah-Keren-Yish'i	Lord the Horn *of* My Salvation	Ps. 18:2
יְהוָה מַחְסִי	Yahowah-Makhesi	Lord My Refuge	Ps. 91:9
יְהוָה מָגֵן	Yahowah-Magen	Lord is Shield (Surrounding)	Deut. 33:29
יְהוָה מַכֶּה	Yahowah-Makeh	Lord Who Strikes You	Ezek. 7:9
יְהוָה מָעֻזִּי	Yahowah-Ma'ozi	Lord is My Fortress	Jer. 16:19
יְהוָה מְנַחֵם	Yahowah-Me'naḥēm	Yahowah My Comforter	Lam 1:10
יְהוָה מְקַדִּשְׁכֶם	Yahowah-Me'qadishkem	Lord Who Makes Them Holy	Exod. 31:13
יְהוָה מֶלֶךְ עוֹלָם וָעֶד	Yahowah-Melech Olam Wa'ed	Lord King Forever and Ever	Ps. 10:16
יְהוָה מְפַלְטִי	Yahowah-Mephalti	Lord My Deliverer	Ps. 18:2
יְהוָה מוֹשִׁיעֵךְ	Yahowah-Moshi'ech	Lord Your Savior	Isa. 49:26; 60:16
יְהוָה נִסִּי	Yahowah-Nissi	Lord My Banner	Exod. 17:15
יְהוָה אוֹרִי	Yahowah-'Ori	Lord My Light	Ps. 27:1
יְהוָה רֹעִי	Yahowah-Rohi	Lord My Shepherd	Ps. 23:1
יְהוָה רֹפְאֶ	Yahowah-Rophe	Lord My Healer	Exod. 15:26
יְהוָה צְבָאוֹת	Yahowah-Sabaoth	The Lord of Hosts	1 Sam. 1:3
יְהוָה סַלְעִי	Yahowah-Sel'i	The Lord My Rock	Ps. 18:2
יְהוָה צִדְקֵנוּ	Yahowah-Tsidkenu	Our Righteousness	Jer. 23:6
יְהוָה	Yahowah-Uzi	My Strength	Ps. 28:7

The above compilation of the Lord יְהוָה name and His authority was authored and originally collocated; Babalobi. He added several Hebrew names and made corrections on the translations and meanings from each scripture. The Lord, Yahowah (יְהֹוָה) is the God of Noah, Shem, Avraham, Yitsak, and Yaccov-who was renamed Isra'el. The Lord's name can be shortened to "Yah" in certain translations, such as Hallelu-Yah.

In Hebrew, numbers and letters have the same multidimensionally enumerated values. For example, Aleph ("א") is numerically the number one, so God is One (Heb. אֶחָד, transl. echad). In English, for example, words are separate from their literary translations. Meaning you must understand several alternate forms of knowledge that are rejected in nature. The singularity of nature rebukes all forms of disunity, and its profound poly-historic or erudite methods are only found in Hebrew. But in the Hebrew language letters formed the stars, the heavens, the sun and moons, and the kingdom; the numeric voice of the Lord, and the mysteries of the biblical Hebrew names. For example, in Genesis and the Book of Creation, the Hebraic letters formed man and all creation. The Aleph and the Tau ("אֵת") are formed in the twenty-two bones on the human skull. It is also the name of God, YHVH in the amino nucleotides that form RNA in all human life. Reading numerically, El'Shaddi ("God Almighty") sits amongst the seven lamp stands and He is the eternal God, if we take the twenty-two ("22") letters and divided by seven ("7"). The seven lamp stands equates to the eternal number pi or tau backwards ("ת" or 3.14).

All of creation and all of life is formed by the very Hebrew words we have lost or been blinded to. For greater clarity, the

Hebrew language, by design, forces us to consider disestablishment for the sake of eliminating confusion and any misappropriations of knowledge, wisdom, seasons and time Why have we not considered that learning and speaking with God *in* His Language would *now* allow us to know His faith even more. Knowing the language eliminates any forms of language appropriation.

But praise be to God, you are not lost anymore and can choose today to learn the language. If a child can learn to talk with their parents through imitating, we also can learn to imitate the great patriarch Avraham and understand the language as well.

The People

In the Book of Amos 9:7 God is speaking to the Isra'elites. "Are ye not as children of the Ethiopians unto me O children of Isra'el, said the Lord," meaning that they were first Ethiopian, originally living in the land of Ethiopia, now currently changed to Hebrew. This next scripture comes from Zechariah 9:13, confirming that Greece was preparing to invade the Black nation of Isra'el, led by Alexander the Great, who invaded Egypt in 332 B.C. This was the start of European dominance for 2,300 years. Another invasion took place by the Roman Empire in 65 B.C., when armies under General Pompey captured Jerusalem. During this period, it was estimated 1,000,000 Isra'elites fled into Africa, fleeing from Roman persecution and slavery. The slave markets were full of Black Isra'elite slaves.

The Enemy Within

A man and his wife were having an argument about who should brew the coffee each morning.

The wife said, "You should do it because you get up first, and then we don't have to wait as long to get our coffee."

The husband said, "You are in charge of cooking around here and you should do it, because that is your job, and I can just wait for my coffee."

The Testament of Mikha'el

The wife replies, "No, you should do it, and besides, it is in the Bible that the man should do the coffee,".

The husband replies, "I can't believe that, show me." So, she fetched the Bible, and opened the New Testament and showed him at the top of several pages, that it indeed says 'HEBREWS' ("Who Should Make the Coffee? - Beliefnet")

Foundational Scripture - Galatians 3:15-27

"I know that nothing good lives in me, that is, in my flesh; for I have the desire to do what is good, but I cannot carry it out. For I do not do the good I want to do. Instead, I keep on doing the evil I do not want to do. And if I do what I do not want, it is no longer I who do it, but it is sin living in me that does it.

So this is the principle I have discovered: When I want to do good, evil is right there with me. For in my inner being I delight in God's Law. But I see another law at work in my body, warring against the law of my mind and holding me captive to the law of sin that dwells within me. What a wretched man I am! Who will rescue me from this body of death? Thanks be to God, through Jesus Christ our Lord!" (Romans 7:18-25)

Personality

Genesis 3 "Now the serpent was more cunning than any beast of the field which the Lord God had made. And he said to the woman, 'Has God indeed said, *You shall not eat of every tree of the garden'?*" And the woman said to the serpent, 'We may eat the fruit of the trees of the garden; but of the fruit of the tree which is in the midst of the garden, God has said, *You shall not eat it, nor shall you touch it, lest you die*.' Then the serpent said to the woman, 'You will not surely die. For God knows that in the day you eat of it your eyes will be opened, and you will be like God, knowing good and evil.' So when the woman saw that the tree was good for food, that it was pleasant to the eyes, and a tree desirable to make one wise, she took of its fruit and ate. She also gave to her husband with her, and he ate. Then the eyes of both of them were opened, and they knew that they were naked." (Genesis 3:1-7)

Seeing is Believing

That the tree was good for food – basic necessity, "I need the basic necessity to live, and clearly God is alright with this..." basic necessity seems worth it in the moment for something less worthy.

"when the boys grew up, Esau became a skillful hunter, a man of the field, but Jacob was a peaceful man, living in tents. Now Isaac loved Esau, because he had a taste for game, but Rebekah loved Jacob. When Jacob had cooked stew, Esau came in from the field and he was famished; and Esau said to Jacob, 'Please let me have a swallow of that red stuff there, for I am famished.' Therefore his name was called Edom. But Jacob said, "First sell me your birthright.' Esau said, 'Behold, I am about to die; so of what use then is the birthright to me?' And Jacob said,

The Testament of Mikha'el

'First swear to me'; so he swore to him, and sold his birthright to Jacob. Then Jacob gave Esau bread and lentil stew; and he ate and drank, and rose and went on his way. Thus Esau despised his birthright." (Gen 25:27-34, 27)

"Then they lifted up their voices and wept again; and Orpah kissed her mother-in-law, but Ruth clung to her. And she said, 'Look, your sister-in-law has gone back to her people and to her gods; return after your sister-in-law.'" (Ruth 1: 14-15)

It was a delight to the eyes a primal attraction, "I can't help it but it looks good so that clearly means God made this tempting" Internal-Lie: The first Lie is the lie we tell ourselves or the lie we want to believe *Keep your tongue from evil, and your lips from speaking deceit. Keep thy heart with all diligence; for out of it are the issues of life.* The tree was to be desired to make one wise – delusional increase. "I desire to rise or increase. God wants this for me." Misplaced war: "Has God indeed said, 'You shall not eat of every tree of the garden'? And the woman said to the serpent, "We may eat the fruit of the trees of the garden;" Flesh is not attacked internally, only externally.

The Big Idea

"For we do not wrestle against flesh and blood, but against principalities, against powers, against the rulers of the darkness of this age, [c] against spiritual hosts of wickedness in the heavenly places. Therefore take up the whole armor of God that you may be able to withstand in the evil day, and having done all, to stand." (Ephesians 6:12-13)

"Not by might nor by power, but by My Spirit,' says the Lord of hosts." (Zechariah 4:6)

"Therefore, submit to God. Resist the devil and he will flee from you'" (Ja4:7)

Always put on the right stuff - "Stand therefore, having girded your waist with truth, having put on the breastplate of righteousness, and having shod your feet with the preparation of the gospel of peace; above all, taking the shield of faith with which you will be able to quench all the fiery darts of the wicked one. And take the helmet of salvation, and the sword of the Spirit, which is the word of God; praying always with all prayer and supplication in the Spirit." (Ephesians 6:14-18)

Stay Positive -[Meditate on These Things]" Finally, brethren, whatever things are true, whatever things are noble, whatever things are just, whatever things are pure, whatever things are lovely, whatever things are of good report, if there is any virtue and if there is anything praiseworthy—meditate on these things." (Philippians 4:8)

Build your life with Goodness and Godliness - let not mercy and truth forsake you; Bind them around your neck, Write them on the tablet of your heart, and so find favor and high esteem. 4 In the sight of God and man. 5 Trust in the Lord with all your heart, and lean not on your own understanding; 6 in all your ways acknowledge Him, And He shall direct[a] your paths." (Proverbs 3:3-4)

See God's promises from His eyes - Ecclesiastes 5:19-20

The Testament of Mikha'el

"Furthermore, as for every man to whom God has given riches and wealth, He has also empowered him to eat from them [a] and to receive his reward [b] and rejoice in his labor[c]; this is a gift of God. 20 For he will not often consider the years of his life[d], because God keeps him occupied with the gladness of his heart[e]." (Ecclesiastes 5:19-20)

"But Ruth said, 'Don't force me to leave you; don't make me go home. Where you go, I go; and where you live, I'll live. Your people are my people, your God is my god; where you die, I'll die, and that's where I'll be buried, so help me God—not even death itself is going to come between us'!" (Ruth 1:16-17)

"Finally, warring against the law of my mind," (Philippians 2:3). For it is God who is at work in you, both to will and to work for His good pleasure." (In other words he's got your back.) Galatians 3:15-27

Eve and Adam, Esau justified what they wanted
    basic necessity
    primal attraction
    delusional increase

The Big Idea:
    No whom you fight
    Always put on the right stuff
    Stay Positive
    Build your life with Goodness and Godliness
    See God's promises from His perspective

Marriage

Remember the words of the Elect One, Jesus, who said it was never to be so that we should put away our spouses. Reading of.

"The Pharisees also came unto him, tempting him, and saying unto him, Is it lawful for a man to put away his wife for every cause? And he answered and said unto them, Have ye not read, that he which made them at the beginning made them male and female, And said, For this cause shall a man leave father and mother, and shall cleave to his wife: and they twain shall be one flesh? Wherefore they are no more twain, but one flesh. What therefore God hath joined together, let not man put asunder. They say unto him, Why did Moses then command to give a writing of divorcement, and to put her away? He saith unto them, Moses because of the hardness of your hearts suffered you to put away your wives: but from the beginning it was not so." (Mathew 19: 3-8)

Are we to love in the way God loves us - in all the challenging ways that loving a spouse may challenge us? I only speak from the side of a Husband of over 20 years, that I come in agreement with the word above, I am also sensitive to the fact that Moses knew that to love the way Jesus loves point is very hard to do. Jesus aspiration is of the greater Law, and many are unable to meet His expectation. But that does not mean God will change the true intention or its original intent because we can't seem to

The Testament of Mikha'el

change in response. This is why Jesus offers us the grace of forgiveness and the mercy to be forgiven. This verse is harsh, but it challenges us as those who have or may be thinking of becoming Husbands -to go as far as you can to love your wives in patience, in forgiveness, as Christ forebear the sins of all the world.

Men, the bible says, that a man who finds a good wife, finds a good thing and obtains favor from God. You must stand boldly and profess that you are willing to take on a wife to others especially if you have family that is before God, mother and friends, you are taking on wife. By doing this God promises that you He will give you favor from Him to be able to overcome all the challenges that being Husband will entail. This is an act of faith I am speaking of and many are unable to do it, but I extol you to be good men, truly, and if you fail in these words don't live in condemnation, but do as so many fathers of faith have done. Get up, repent, and say God I can do better. "For a righteous man may fall seven times and rise again, But the wicked shall fall by calamity." (Proverbs 24:16) Being righteous is about never giving up on the faith you believe, and knowing God has your back on surviving almost anything.

"Wives, submit yourselves to your own husbands as you do to the Lord. For the husband is the head of the wife as Christ is the head of the church, his body, of which he is the Savior. Now as the church submits to Christ, so also wives should submit to their husbands in everything." (Ephesians 5:22-33 New International Version (NIV)

Enough said, oh wives and those desiring to be wives in this generation, learn the discipline of knowing the truth by helping your husband become what you see for you and your family. He may carry the vision, but you, oh wives of good character and faithfulness, carry his dreams to fulness. I expound this to you only that you may prove to become lovely to one another and remember that the choice of marriage is yours, so, if possible, choose wisely.

I extol you both men and women that are looking for a spouse, if its possible use family and godly men and women to help create accountability for yourself and your spouse, again choose wisely.

State of Confusion

At some point I had to deal with what America, under the guidance of the fourteenth amendment, did to the law; to allow a people to have the right to due process under the law, regardless of the nature of its unions. So here are my thoughts to really simple issue. Before the laws were changed to allow alternate parings of disingenuous groups-they could not receive due process of law, because they had no legal ground to bring suit into the court in defense of practices associated with legal union. Religious institutions refused the aforementioned unions; this right of due process on the grounds that homogenous sexual preference created unions broken from the conscience of the God of Israel's law regarding homosexual relationships; thereby breaking the tents of state law. The problem is "as the legal State", refusing said individuals the right of due process under law joined those group of similar relationships to a definitional word, "Marriage" which would be a missed *right* to the same.

So then, what must a judgement committed to; that upon enforcement at supreme measure by not finding a more equitable way to reduce the harm caused by the perceptions, and facts of elevated privileges afforded to a pairing group that could not be in the confines of "Marriage?"

That being exclusively a part of an elevated pairing group, they could receive no rights under the law afforded by other pairings. So now all are in violation of discrimination because a disenfranchised pairing group could not receive elevated rights and the governed pairings, under due process, could receive that which another type of pairing cannot receive.

The challenge is that the United States Supreme Court ultimately had to refused to rule on the dismantling of pairing groups who received elevate rights. For all others, the judicial branch had no legal grounds to write laws to determine which pairing should receive benefits, and could not alter the law established by congress on the legal basis of how it should perceive legal privileges applied; (as in taxation or estate transfers), the court was by prudence forced by due process to allow any pairing group to legally receive this right intended for all groups. The challenge with this intent is that the court was forced to elevate this group to the same rights previously held exclusively by "Marriage" between man and woman pairings as all are unionization in order to not violate the law. Leaving the definition of unionization to any pairing of homologous groups of sound conscience and legal age to enter into contract. Now "Marriage" as the definition of the word is irrevocably redefined by the state and the institution, is defined by this law change.

The People

The challenge is not a 282AD year institution of the common law of "Marriage" which is owned and must now be redefined by the courts for all. If the court's system must now redefine the definition of the word "Marriage," it violates the law of conscience for those groups who are the originators, perverts its use of the same as defined law in religious expressions when using the word unionization (of the Ur-Nammu or Babylonian law word for "Marriage,") between common or traditional man and woman pronouns.

The 14th Amendment of the United States Constitution guarantees that no state will be able to "deprive any person of life, liberty, or property, without due process of law." This amendment ensures that every person, regardless of race, ethnicity, or sexual orientation, has the right to due process under the law. However, the controversy regarding the rights of same-sexed couples in relation to marriage began to violate due process in egregious partisan in the medical, legal, and in executorial requirements after death.

With the same manner of judicial pressure, the Christian institutions, at the time of creation, defined by precedence of the courts of Israel in Leviticus 18:22, "You shall not lie with a male as with a woman; it is an abomination.", was reduced in its prominence to the State.

In the New Testament, Romans 1:26-27 reads, "For this reason God gave them up to dishonorable passions. For their women exchanged natural relations for those that are contrary to nature; and the men likewise gave up natural relations with women and were consumed with passion for one another, men committing shameless acts with men and receiving in themselves the due penalty for their error."

The Testament of Mikha'el

So, what conclusion must we draw upon to govern ourselves in a righteous matter when America pursues in the foundation of an easing from the foundation of Isra'el's moral law? I would look to the onset of the Lord's servant Lot for a valid comparison.

The story of Lot, found in the book of Genesis according to the King James Version of the Bible, begins with Lot and his family living in the city of Sodom, known for its wickedness and sinfulness. Genesis 13:13 (KJV) states, "But the men of Sodom were wicked and sinners before the Lord exceedingly."

To provide a witness of this wickedness, Jeremiah 23:14 gives an indication of the sins in Sodom. "I have seen also in the prophets of Jerusalem a horrible thing: they commit adultery, and walk in lies: they strengthen also the hands of evildoers, that none doth return from his wickedness: they are all of them unto me as Sodom, and the inhabitants thereof as Gomorrah." But why? According to the book of Jasher 19, the daughter of Lot, Paltith, was judged by wicked judges of Sodom for giving bread to a poor man and the judgement cast claimed that she broke their laws. Then she was sentenced to be burned. This was the first witness. Again, another women who acted similar to Paltith was judged and sentenced her to death for serving a poor man. This was accounted for in the Book of Jasher, Chapter 19:42-44.

"And the people of those cities assembled and brought out the young woman, and anointed her with honey from head to foot, as the judge had decreed, and they placed her before a swarm of bees which were then in their hives, and the bees flew upon her and stung her that her whole body was swelled. And the young woman cried out on account of the bees, but no one took notice of her or

pitied her, and her cries ascended to heaven. And the Lord was provoked at this and at all the works of the cities of Sodom, for they had abundance of food, and had tranquility amongst them, and still would not sustain the poor and the needy, and in those days their evil doings and sins became great before the Lord."
(Book of Jasher 19:42-44)

This law was so unrighteous that the consciousness of moral imperatives unabated led to a shameless violation of the higher law, more excellently than all on the earth and summarized by Galatian 5: 22-23, "But the fruit of the Spirit is love, joy, peace, patience, kindness, goodness, faithfulness, gentleness, and self-control. Against such things there is no law." Their perversion of justice cemented the cause of the second witness and fulfilled the law, as it is written in Deuteronomy 17:6 and Deuteronomy 19:15.

The path of unrighteous law, in its simplest form of perversion, will at some point, if not repudiated by both Judges and its people, will lead to the state's madness of the greater law. God's decision to destroy Sodom, and the neighboring cities of Gomorrah, was because their perversion was against the greater law of doing good. This was the second witness.

The story of Lot serves as a warning of the consequences of judges and its people's agreement to pervert the Gospel of peace in Galatians and the Torah for the convenience of state's laws. Any agreement to sin and disobedience to Yahowah will lead to the state perverting the law of martial obedience and will inevitably lead to perversion in all judgement and martial disobedience in the furtherance to perversion of all homogenous groups.

In summary, the whole statement argues that the path of unrighteousness, characterized by perversion and a departure from the greater law of doing good, will eventually lead to a state of madness and destruction if not rejected by both judges and the people. It references the biblical story of Sodom and Gomorrah, where God's decision to destroy these cities was based on their perversion and departure from the greater law. The story of Lot is presented as a warning against perverting the Gospel and the Torah for the convenience of state laws; suggesting that any agreement to sin and disobedience to God will lead to the state perverting martial obedience and judgment, ultimately resulting in perversion among all homogenous groups.

The Witnesses Against Sodom and Gomorrah	
First Witness	Second Witness
Lot's daughter Paltith (פלט, in the root Etymology palat, def. "means to bring into security, cause to escape, or to deliver.") disobeys the law and is killed for showing compassion to the poor.	A woman arrives in the provinces of Admah (Heb. אֲדָמָה, def. "red, ruddy earth"), one of the five cities of the Vale of Siddim, and is killed for showing acts of compassion to the poor.
Paltith is stateman that knowingly breaks the law to show love to strangers.	A stranger unpracticed in the laws of the local community or province is sentenced to death for doing an act of kindness to a stranger.

Michael's Wisdom.

The perversion of the "greater measure" outlined in Galatians 5, will make room for any kind of wickedness, and set its reign against the supreme reign of moral conscience. Then the cause and case of judgements, and the people in agreement; will bear witness to its perversion, thereby judging themselves. The Lord will defend harshly against this type of perversion.

Death requires more than one witness. At the mouth of two witnesses, or three witnesses, shall he that is worthy of death be put to death; but at the mouth of one witness, he shall not be put to death. (Deuteronomy 17:6)	**Any appointed punishment for breaking Torah must have more than one witness.** One witness shall not rise up against a man for any *punishment for* iniquity, or for any sin, in any sin that he sinneth: at the mouth of two witnesses, or at the mouth of three witnesses, shall the matter be established. (Deuteronomy 19:15)

The Greater Measure. But the fruit of the Spirit is love, joy, peace, patience, kindness, goodness, faith, gentleness, and self-control. ***Against such things there is no law***. Galatian 5: 22-23.

The Testament of Mikha'el

In conclusion, I am leaving with the interpretation by a powerful statement and address made by Alan Keys' on the principle of marriage in an interview:

> *An individual who is impotent or another who is infertile does not change the definition of marriage in principle because between a man and a woman in principle, procreation is always possible. And it is that possibility which gave rise to the institution of marriage in the first place. As a matter of law, possible in principle. But when it is impossible, as between two males or two females, you're talking about something that's not just incidentally impossible, it's impossible in principle. And that means that if you say that that's a marriage you are saying marriage can be understood in principle apart from procreation, you have changed its definition in such a way as in fact to destroy the necessity for the institution since the only reason it has existed in human societies and civilizations was to regulate from a social point of view the obligations and responsibilities attendant upon procreation.* (Keys, 2004)

As a point of fact, if you don't own the term, you can't redefine it on a whim whenever you want to. If the route of unrighteousness, which is marked by perversion and a divergence from the larger law of doing good, is not rejected by both the judges and the people, the entire statement argues that it will eventually lead to a condition of lunacy and ruin. My references on the biblical tale of Sodom and Gomorrah, in which

God's decision to destroy these towns, was based on the fact that they had perverted the larger law and strayed from it. It is suggested that any agreement to sin and disobedience to God will lead to the state perverting martial obedience and judgment, which will ultimately result in perversion among all homogenous groups, and this is why the story of Lot is presented as a warning against perverting the Gospel and the Torah for the convenience of state laws. Succinctly, the story of Lot is presented as a warning against perverting the Gospel and the Torah for the convenience of state laws.

Prayer

Shema is a specific prayer associated with Moses in Deuteronomy, where he commanded Isra'el to continually pray. It is the daily prayer quoted in the morning and evening according to Psalms 55:17, and since the days of Daniel (דָּנִיֵּאל, def. "God is my Judge") and the 3 Isra'elite men, Hananiah (חֲנַנְיָה, def. "God has favored"), Mishael (מִישָׁאֵל, def. "Who is what God is"), and Azariah (וַעֲזַרְיָה, def. "Yahowah has helped").

The Shema begins with the fundamental expressions of love, and the one from which this prayer gets its name: Shema Yisra'el. (שְׁמַע יִשְׂרָאֵל, def. "Hear, Isra'el"). The biblical expression adds the importance of the hearts and minds to the twenty-two (22) letters of creation to be as one. The next part comes from Deuteronomy 11:13-21 and adds the promise of rewards for obedience and condemnation for sin. The final blessing of the Shema is in Numbers 15:37-41. It references wearing tzitzit

The Testament of Mikha'el

(fringes) on the clothing of the priest of Aaron and the Holy people as a reminder of the commandments. This passage includes the mitzvah to remember the Exodus from the first Egypt ("Kemet") and the last Egypt ("the diaspora of Isra'el").

DEUTERONOMY 6:4-9

4שְׁמַע יִשְׂרָאֵל יְהוָה אֱלֹהֵינוּ יְהוָה אֶחָד׃

Shema Yisra'eil Yahowah Elohenu Yahowah Echad:

"Hear, Isra'el, the Lord is our God, the Lord is One:"

5וְאָהַבְתָּ אֵת יְהוָה אֱלֹהֶיךָ בְּכָל־לְבָבְךָ וּבְכָל־נַפְשְׁךָ וּבְכָל־מְאֹדֶךָ׃

we'ahave'ta et Yahowah Elohekha b'kal-l'vav'kha uv'cal-nafesh'kha uv'cal-m'odekha:

"And thou shalt love, twenty-two Hebraic letters ("the language of creation"), Yahowah your God with all your heart, and with all your soul, and with all your might:"

6וְהָיוּ הַדְּבָרִים הָאֵלֶּה אֲשֶׁר אָנֹכִי מְצַוְּךָ הַיּוֹם עַל־לְבָבֶךָ׃

wᵊhāyû hadbārîm hā'ēllê ăšher ānōḵî mᵊṣaûᵊḵā hayyôm 'al lᵊbābeḵā:

"And these words, which I command you this day, will be in your heart:"

The People

7:וְשִׁנַּנְתָּם לְבָנֶיךָ וְדִבַּרְתָּ בָּם בְּשִׁבְתְּךָ בְּבֵיתֶךָ וּבְלֶכְתְּךָ בַדֶּרֶךְ וּבְשָׁכְבְּךָ וּבְקוּמֶךָ:

"And you will teach them diligently unto your children, and will talk of them when you sit in your house, and when you walk by the way, and when you lie down, and when you rise up:"

8וּקְשַׁרְתָּם לְאוֹת עַל־יָדֶךָ וְהָיוּ לְטֹטָפֹת בֵּין עֵינֶיךָ:

"And thou shalt bind them for a sign upon thine hand, and they shall be as frontlets between thine eyes."

9וּכְתַבְתָּם עַל־מְזוּזֹת בֵּיתֶךָ וּבִשְׁעָרֶיךָ: ס

"And thou shalt write them upon the posts of thy house, and on thy gates."

The Aaronic Blessing

This is a blessing that the priests or the Cohenim recite over the people, blessing God by blessing them. It is found in Numbers 6:24-26:

The Testament of Mikha'el

יְבָרֶכְךָ יְהוָה וְיִשְׁמְרֶךָ׃

yə·ḇā·reḵ·ḵā YHWH wə·yiš·mə·re·ḵā

"May Yahowah bless you and keep you;"

יָאֵר יְהוָה ׀ פָּנָיו אֵלֶיךָ וִיחֻנֶּךָּ׃

yā·'êr YHWH pā·nāw 'ê·le·ḵā wî·ḥun·ne·kā

"May the Yahowah make His face shine upon you and be gracious to you;"

יִשָּׂא יְהוָה ׀ פָּנָיו אֵלֶיךָ וְיָשֵׂם לְךָ שָׁלוֹם׃

yiś·śā YHWH pā·nāw 'ê·le·ḵā wə·yā·śêm le·ḵā šā·lō·wm

"May the Yahowah lift up His countenance toward you and grant you peace."

The Sabbath

"Remember the sabbath day, to keep it holy. Six days shalt thou labour, and do all thy work: But the seventh day [is] the sabbath of the LORD thy God: [in it] thou shalt not do any work, thou, nor thy son, nor thy daughter, thy manservant, nor thy maidservant, nor thy cattle, nor thy stranger that [is] within thy gates: For [in] six days the LORD made heaven and earth, the sea, and all that in them [is], and rested the seventh day: wherefore the LORD blessed the sabbath day, and hallowed it." (Exodus 20:8-11)

The People

וְהִתְעַנַּג עַל־יְהוָה וְיִתֶּן־לְךָ מִשְׁאֲלֹת לִבֶּךָ

"Delight thyself also in the LORD; and he shall give thee the desires of thine heart."
(Psalms 37:4)

אִם־תָּשִׁיב מִשַּׁבָּת רַגְלֶךָ עֲשׂוֹת חֲפָצֶיךָ בְּיוֹם קָדְשִׁי וְקָרָאתָ לַשַּׁבָּת עֹנֶג לִקְדוֹשׁ יְהוָה מְכֻבָּד וְכִבַּדְתּוֹ מֵעֲשׂוֹת דְּרָכֶיךָ מִמְּצוֹא חֶפְצְךָ וְדַבֵּר דָּבָר:

"If you turn away your foot from the sabbath, doing your pleasure on my holy day; and call the sabbath a delight, the holy of the LORD, honorable; and will honor him, not doing thine own ways, nor finding thine own pleasure, nor speaking thine own words: Then shalt thou delight thyself in the LORD; and I will cause thee to ride upon the high places of the earth, and feed thee with the heritage of Jacob thy father: for the mouth of the LORD hath spoken it."(Isaiah 58:13-14)

The phrase also, "delight yourself in the Lord" is found in the Bible in Psalm 37:4 in the King James Version (KJV): "Delight thyself also in the Lord: and he shall give thee the desires of thine heart."

This passage encourages us in the application of Shabbat, in-turn, showing outwardly a delight in the Lord and finding joy in doing and practicing our relationship with Him. When we set our mind and heart to living our life for God, we please Him above all else, He is faithful to response to His promises to bless or edify the doers with the desires of our hearts. So instead of a very broad ungrounded message that could mean almost anything, using Isaiah 58 paired with Psalms 37, this brings a full understanding of the scriptures.

From my wife's wisdom: "Try your best not to argue with your spouse on Shabbat. You may not understand, if you are married or have a significant person in your life, that we are trying to live a life of holiness. The hardest part for women is learning to prepare for Shabbat. On Shabbat you are allowing others to have the freedom to worship God by giving them a day of rest. So, no buying or selling items, if at all possible, on Shabbat, means you are freeing God's people from working. I know that many people today still must go to work on Shabbat, but ask the Lord to show you when God might allow you to be free on Saturday. Again, no compulsion, we can all do this better."

Shabbat Times and Seasons

"And it came to pass, that when the gates of Jerusalem began to be dark before the sabbath, I commanded that the gates should be shut, and charged that they should not be opened till after the sabbath: and some of my servants set I at the gates, that there should no burden be brought in on the sabbath day. So the merchants and sellers of all kind of ware lodged without Jerusalem once or twice." (Nehemiah 19:13-14)

The People

"It shall be unto you a sabbath of rest, and ye shall afflict your souls: in the ninth day of the month at even, from even unto even, shall ye celebrate your sabbath." (Leviticus 23:32). Shabbat starts on **Friday sundown** (evening) to **Saturday sundown** (evening) in your time zones.

Song Sung On Shabbat

"A Psalm [or] Song for the sabbath day.
[It is a] good [thing] to give thanks unto the LORD, and to sing praises unto thy name, O Most High:
To shew forth thy lovingkindness in the morning, and thy faithfulness every night.
Upon an instrument of ten strings, and upon the psaltery; upon the harp with a solemn sound.
For thou, LORD, hast made me glad through thy work: I will triumph in the works of thy hands.
O LORD, how great are thy works! [and] thy thoughts are very deep.
A brutish man knoweth not; neither doth a fool understands this.
When the wicked spring as the grass, and when all the workers of iniquity do flourish; [it is] that they shall be destroyed forever:
But thou, LORD, [art most] high for evermore.
For, lo, thine enemies, O LORD, for, lo, thine enemies shall perish; all the workers of iniquity shall be scattered.
But my horn shalt thou exalt like [the horn of] an unicorn: I shall be anointed with fresh oil.

The Testament of Mikha'el

Mine eye also shall see [my desire] on mine enemies, [and] mine ears shall hear [my desire] of the wicked that rise up against me. The righteous shall flourish like the palm tree: he shall grow like a cedar in Lebanon.
Those that be planted in the house of the LORD shall flourish in the courts of our God.
They shall still bring forth fruit in old age; they shall be fat and flourishing;
To shew that the LORD [is] upright: [he is] my rock, and [there is] no unrighteousness in him." Psalms 92:1-15 (KJV)

In conclusion, the passage stresses the importance of observing Shabbat, showing directly our delight in the Lord and strengthening our relationship with Him. By setting our hearts and minds on living for God, we can expect blessings and edification from Him. The passage also provides practical advice for observing Shabbat, such as avoiding arguments and refraining from buying or selling items, which allows others to have the freedom to worship God. Additionally, the passage acknowledges that not everyone may be able to observe Shabbat in the same way but encourages everyone to do their best. Finally, the passage highlights the importance of using scripture to gain a full understanding of the message.

The Appoint Feast Days

There are several appointed feast days mentioned in the Bible that were given by God to the Isra'elites to celebrate throughout the year. These feasts had both historical and prophetic significance and were intended to remind the Isra'elites of God's faithfulness and provision.

Passover (Pesach): This is the first of the three pilgrimage feasts and is celebrated in the spring. It commemorates the Isra'elites' deliverance from slavery in Egypt. The feast was instituted by God in Exodus 12:1-14. The date for Passover is the 14th day of the first month of the Hebrew calendar, which usually falls in March or April. The celebration of Passover involves the sacrifice and eating of a lamb, the removal of all leaven from the home, and the telling of the story of the Exodus from Egypt. The Isra'elites were commanded to sacrifice a lamb and mark their doorposts with its blood, and the Angel of Death passed over their homes, sparing their firstborn. Jesus is seen as the Passover Lamb who was sacrificed for the sins of humanity, and His blood covers those who believe in Him, protecting them from the judgment of God. Scriptural reference: Exodus 12:1-28, Leviticus 23:4-8, Deuteronomy 16:1-8.

Feast of Unleavened Bread (Chag HaMatzot): The Feast of Unleavened Bread follows immediately after Passover and lasts for seven days. It is also called the Feast of Matzot or the Festival of Bread without Yeast. The feast was instituted by God in Exodus 12:15-20. The purpose of the feast was to remind the Isra'elites of their hasty departure from Egypt and to remove all leaven from their homes. During the Feast of Unleavened Bread, the Isra'elites would eat unleavened bread and avoid all leavened foods. The Feast of Unleavened Bread commemorated the Isra'elites' hasty departure from Egypt and the unleavened bread they had to eat during their journey. Jesus is seen as the bread of life, and His body was broken for us, making a way for us to have eternal life. Scriptural reference: Exodus 12:15-20, Leviticus 23:6-8, Deuteronomy 16:3-4.

Feast of Firstfruits (Yom HaBikkurim): The Feast of Firstfruits was celebrated on the day after the Sabbath following Passover. It marked the beginning of the barley harvest in Israel. The feast was instituted by God in Leviticus 23:9-14. The celebration of the Feast of Firstfruits involved bringing the first sheaf of the barley harvest to the priest as an offering to God. The Isra'elites were commanded to bring the firstfruits of their harvest to the temple as an offering to God. Jesus is seen as the firstfruits of the resurrection, and His resurrection guarantees that we too will be raised in newness of life. Scriptural reference: Leviticus 23:9-14.

Feast of Weeks (Shabu'ot or Shavout): The Feast of Weeks marked the end of the wheat harvest in Israel. The feast was instituted by God: This feast was held fifty days after Passover and celebrated the giving of the Law to Moses on Mount Sinai. It was also a celebration of the wheat harvest. In the New Testament, the Holy Spirit was poured out on the disciples on the day of Pentecost, marking the beginning of the church age. Jesus is seen as the fulfillment of the Law, and the Holy Spirit empowers us to live out God's commands. Scriptural reference: Exodus 34:22-23, Leviticus 23:15-22, Deuteronomy 16:9-12.

Feast of Trumpets (Yom Teruah): The Feast of Trumpets is celebrated on the first day of the seventh month of the Hebrew calendar. It is also known as Rosh Hashanah, which means "head of the year." The feast was instituted by God in Leviticus 23:23-25. During the Feast of Trumpets, Isra'elites blow trumpets and observe a day of rest. This feast is held on the first day of the seventh month. It is a day of blowing trumpets and Jesus is seen as the fulfillment of the trumpet blasts that will sound in judgement upon His return. Scriptural reference: Leviticus 23:23-25, Numbers 29:1-6.

Day of Atonement (Yom Kippur): The Day of Atonement, also known as Yom Kippur, is celebrated on the tenth day of the seventh month of the Hebrew calendar. It was the most solemn and holy day of the year for the Isra'elites.

The purpose of the day was to atone for the sins of the people and to make things right with God. The feast was instituted by God in Leviticus 23:26-32. During the Day of Atonement, the high priest would make sacrifices and offer prayers for the forgiveness of the sins of the people. Jesus is seen in this feast as the ultimate high priest who made atonement for our sins through His death on the cross. Scriptural reference: Leviticus 16, Leviticus 23:26-32.

Feast of Tabernacles or Booths (Sukkot): The Feast of Tabernacles, also known as the Feast of Booths or Sukkot, was celebrated in the fall, five days after the Day of Atonement. The feast was instituted by God in Leviticus 23:33-43. During the Feast of Tabernacles, the Isra'elites would build temporary booths (sukkot) and dwell in them for seven days.

The purpose of the feast is so that people would construct dwellings called sukkahs and live in them for the duration of the festival. This feast is held in the fall and commemorates Isra'elites' forty years of wandering in the wilderness. They lived in temporary booths (or tabernacles) during this time, and the feast is a reminder of God's provision and protection during their journey. Jesus is the Word made flesh, dwelling among us. He is also the fulfillment of the feast, as He will one day establish His

The Testament of Mikha'el

Kingdom on earth and dwell among His people forever. Scriptural reference: Leviticus 23:33-43, Deuteronomy 16:13-15.

Overall, these feast days provide a rich tapestry of meaning that point to Jesus' fulfillment of Law of God's plan for humanity. Each feast highlights a different aspect of Jesus' character and work, and they provide a powerful reminder of God's faithfulness and provision throughout history.

ת Final Thoughts

As we come near to my few and final thoughts, it is my hope that you have already gained a deeper understanding of the God of the Bible and His plan for His people. Throughout the pages, we have explored the significance of the Hebrew language, the importance of returning to the land of יְהוָֹה, and the need to follow God's laws. In these final thoughts, my delightful wife Christina wanted to share a few thoughts with you on her journey in His truth first and then I will close with a thoughtful exercise that will help you know how to hang on to God truth.

Christina's Thoughts to You:

My husband the novelist, Michael Arnwine, asked me to write a few words on the path we've taken together to better health over the past several years. I close my eyes and try to remember where to start; I'm at a loss. In August 2020, after eating some takeout, I got an excruciating stomachache for no apparent reason. My husband brought me to the nearest Methodist Urgent Care Clinic while my mom was in town seeing her grandkids. When they saw my blood count, they were taken aback by how severely anemic I was.

Final Thoughts

That's why I calmly responded to the doctors' questions about my past and my family's health. It wasn't until I started opening up that I realized I was in an interrogation room. I was taken aback by the news. It was at this time that I was alone in the hospital, receiving information from physicians and my husband who couldn't be present to assist me in making judgments because of the chaos that was Covid; which had just begun and was extremely active. I wasn't the healthiest eater, but we were making great strides in the area of nutrition. And so it was that I found myself sitting on the bed, wailing in dread - for anyone who tells you not to be frightened is speaking a lie. After hearing those words, I was hospitalized for a few days, and it felt like I had been given a death sentence.

The discomfort wasn't eased by the physicians, so I anticipated having to make tough decisions in the near future. Both treatment and surgery had failed to assist my sister, *and* my father's colon cancer. Years later, my father's cancer reappeared, leading to his death. That's why I opted for a more all-encompassing diet and lifestyle that day, which would include removing all sugar (it is the major substance that helps cancer develop and thrive in a person's body).

When I got home, I immediately began discarding all the food that I knew would not help me in the process while on this road to healing. This was effective for almost two and a half years. I started praying and reading the Bible more to figure out what God wanted me to do with my life. I also started eating better and using holistic diets that helped me go from a size 16 to a size 6 or 8 in a matter of 3 months. This isn't something to be taken lightly, especially given that I'm responsible for three young children and a husband.

The Testament of Mikha'el

I knew that my mother couldn't afford to lose a third kid after she'd already lost two. I knew I had to keep fighting this struggle in my head every day. Furthermore, via my own private Bible study, this experience brought me closer to God; more than I had ever been before. I walked outside after a night of rain, got down on my knees, and prayed like I never prayed before, all in an effort to better understand, His guidelines, procedures, and laws.

The Lord needed me to question Him humbly, "Where are you, Lord? I require your presence."

No matter what you do, it may appear you're on your own, but you have to continue to fight and pray.

A friend of mine inquired if I had heard of a center in Mexico called Hope for Cancer that provides holistic therapy for people with cancer. My husband and I traveled to this clinic in Cancun, Mexico that specializes holistic therapy. I felt fantastic, in spite of the cancer. I knew that when the three weeks were done, life would go back to normal, with all its blessings and difficulties. With God's help, trying to manage life, kids, husband, and now my at home treatments, life was difficult at times but I remembered it was/is possible. One of the things I remind the Lord on a daily basis is "I'm doing as much as I can, take what I'm doing, and you do the rest times a million."

God has been an ever-present pillar of stability for me and my husband. I don't know what I would've done if our family wasn't observing Shabbat weekly. Shabbat is a life saver for us. I don't believe we would have made it through what we've gone through, and are currently going through without it. In the

Final Thoughts

midst of treating the cancer, my anemia was treated with weekly transfusions and my hemoglobin is back to normal today.

Moreover, I will include, I'm happy He prepared me with the doctor my friend recommended. His positive attitude and reassuring words put me at rest. I realized I needed to take greater measures since, as I said previously, what I was doing was minimizing the situation but not curing it.

I've had many people pray over me; still waiting on the Lord to answer those prayers. This is when my husband began to look into the scriptures more deeply looking for some answers. I began to encourage myself in the Lord and developed a desire to know what His word said for myself.

With everything, you just want to know that you will survive to see your kids grow up; that you were healed by the wounds He sustained; that Jesus Christ is the same yesterday, today, and forever; and that you have been given a second chance at life. I want to share the good news of what God has done. This is the hardest thing I've ever had to go through, and it's not easy, but I am confident that this experience will make me a better person overall.

You have to understand deep down that there are mornings when I awake in such excruciating pain that I require medication just to get out of bed and walk around with my baby. Some mornings I have a hard time getting out of bed, and if I don't have anybody to push me out of bed, I can stay there all day. But the Lord is reliable, kind, and all-knowing. The future is so unpredictable that I can't say for sure if we'll live or die. His word says that we are not promised tomorrow.

The Testament of Mikha'el

If I'm in pain or finding it difficult to get out of bed, I tell myself that God's ways are higher than our ways and His thoughts are higher than our thoughts, and that helps me get out of bed and start my day.

Although modern science has equipped doctors with powerful tools to fight cancer, the public still may have little faith in them. *So, Lord, please let this be the generation in which the curse is lifted.* Besides making me well again and to continue my previous point, I do occasionally read about Job and his ordeals. It's natural to feel emotional, and tears are no excuse not to put up a fight. Put up some effort to reclaim your joy. Hang in there. You'll be able to show the Lord, to make it known to him, that you are still willing to work through it. I know that when I do, I will be able to tell you what the Lord has done, and I trust that hearing it will fortify your desire to cling to Him and His Word. You shouldn't give up the fight because it isn't happening right now.

However, our only chance of survival is in God, His Truth, and His Light. If you want to make it through this, you have to stop acting like a victim. I'm writing this down so that maybe someone else might learn from my experience and not make the same mistakes I made. Trust in the Lord. Your story is yours to write. Try your best not to be discouraged through your journey. Remember what His word says in Hebrews 12:6 "For whom the Lord loves He chastens, And scourges every son whom He receives." In knowing this scripture, it reminds me daily that the Lord loves me. He is the same yesterday, today, and forever more. By dying on the cross, Jesus demonstrated that God could do the seemingly impossible, so welcome to the impossible!

Michael's Final Thoughts

What remains is the question that was posed to Yahoshua during His wilderness experience, and maybe at one time was proposed to you. Why would the adversary or to Baal (the ways of the adversary) ask the Lord His God such a dangerous question like, "If you would bow your knee and worship me?"

The reason why he could ask that question to the Most High, to his God, was because I understand the purpose of that question. His temptation should have been said a little bit differently, a little bit deeper. But maybe the words in Hebrew did not exist. It was not a temptation only, but an approach that meant He would be able to take something that wasn't given. You see Jesus believe in the impossible and that His bride and all of her harshness; and in her confusion, and her desire to want something now instead of waiting a millennia for Him. And in all these years Jesus was now on the Earth in order to speak directly to His bride Isra'el. Imagine the level of commitment and time it took to keep His bride alive these many years. The level in the strength of faith a person has to have that speaks out, "she will be mine." This is the complexity of our God. This is the complexity of this faith. But He would say, "she will be mine."

Though I slay her through rejection and blind Isra'el that they never return to their formal glory in Malachi, the Lord reiterates the statement, "Isra'el will be mine." A complexity, and felt eventuality that Jesus had to endure this ungodly, wicked taunting in the wilderness of perdition.

The Testament of Mikha'el

That you would never reach your goals. That you would never see the glorious return of Isra'el. And the adversary, in testing Jesus, reminding him of the stiffness of His people.

But Jesus, full of faith, didn't answer his question like an earthly bride groom, He answered the adversary in His submission to the humility of God. Thus, reminding the adversary of His subjugation to the Words of God. That by your tongue, you are not allowed to tempt the Lord your God who made you. 'How can you know more than me?' was the question. He didn't only rebuke the devil, He reminded him of the truth. You see, your bible and this book is a reminder of the truth. And truth is neither hard nor soft, evil or good; it doesn't care about pain or the need for love; it's just the truth.

As I was praying about the conclusion of this book, the Lord placed in me a heart of compassion and love for all His people. As it is written, without love, many people would be lost to sin because they cannot find God. They are looking in every form for the example of Love and are unable to find it. Many are even sacrificing righteous living for love. But my hope is that this book shows you the breadth and depth of a man named Jesus, who is also called the Truth, who did not sacrifice a momentary desire for His bride for the sake of giving up the Truth. This is the true understanding of sin. Will you sacrifice godliness and this life's momentary gift of companionship, even if that love breaks the Law? For love's sake many have broken, and will you break the Law of Truth? If I lie to you and I have relationships outside of the word of God and feel free to engage in all forms of sexual perversion and fill your cup to engage in all manners of confusion; then I would lie to you in all manners. But at what cost?

Final Thoughts

I was asked a question from the adversary, "If I could heal your wife who is afflicted with various ailments, would you bow your knee to me?"

I pondered the question and considered how I might answer the adversary. For these two years I have suffered, watching violence all around her. I remember this question was asked of Jesus, the one who became flesh for us, was asked by His adversary.

"Will you give up your right to gain her? Will you give up this momentary affliction, the truth, to keep her here? If you are her husband, don't you deserve to be happy? It's a simple question. You only have to do one thing," he said. "You would have to take your knee to the ground, lift your hands in submission to me."

And answering this question in the same way Jesus did. "If Balaam, the wicked priest, could not deny the truth that the Holy people are Isra'el, and to only be blessed, then how could His faithful servant do less? Would I commit my knee to the ground? Would I take this world's opportunity to fast-track the blessing as Sarah and Avraham did with Hagar? Where would I go; to the doors of sexual perversion and adulterers or through the door of the occult? I would then need to agree to become Nebuchadnezzar, an ancient King who went into madness," I responded.

The adversary asks the second time, "It's not much to bend, you don't even need to speak or proclaim your commitment, only demonstrate your ability to bow."

Would you do it for the sake of the gains in this world? For in this present age, the adversary has become strong, full of riches, their barns are filled with all manner of things. To receive their

The Testament of Mikha'el

glory comes from bowing the knee. Would you bow your knee? How easy it would be to allow those sinews, those muscles, those decisions to just bow. Don't speak, don't consider your ways, only bow the knee.

Aren't you tired? After 5783 years of suffering, Isra'el or the former enslaved. Aren't you tired, Isra'el, of being subjugated to slavery many times and subjected to police brutality? Aren't you tired of watching your wives suffering many pains or undergoing the loss of your little ones? Aren't you tired of never feeling safe to venture outside both night and day? Aren't you tired of subjugation, even to God and all His 613 laws? What profits a man to continue in the ways of the Most High? When the lamenting going on in Malachi was heard by the Lord Jesus, He said by faith you will be mine. Even at the point of the end of the prophets, He said you will be mine. You're capable of gaining freedom, and all you have to do is hold fast to your faith as David was when he was being chased by His father-in-law.

In Psalms 91, it says, "only with eyes shall you look, and see the reward of the wicked" This was happening after all David had gone through. And I can see a future where David's story will be repeated again. That those afflicted for over 400 years of injustice without repair or due process will observe the wickedness of two parties undergoing a hidden battle of whiteness and the ongoing attempt to return to subjugation of His people. So where could you go now? Sit back people of the Most High, *sit back now, Michael*, sit back and only observed. The Lord your God will complete a new Exodus dealing with cancer and all various kinds of diseases.

For the children of God will be guided to their return, to their roots, to the ways of their forefathers, and to the teachings of the

Final Thoughts

Torah. Through the guidance of the Holy Spirit, we can boldly approach God's laws, statutes, Shabbats, and Appointed Feast Days without feeling compelled or forced. Instead, we can embrace these practices with joy and faith; knowing that they are intended to bring us closer to God and to help us lead lives that are pleasing to Him.

One of the key themes of this book is the importance of the priesthood within the kingdom of Isra'el and the reinstatement of His judges for the remission of sin. We have explored the biblical basis for these teachings and seen how they are essential to the proper functioning of God's people. By following these practices, we can become more effective ambassadors of God's kingdom and more effective witnesses to the world around us. The revelation of the diaspora's return to the judicial governances, times, and seasons of God is now come. The restoration of these practices is essential to the fulfillment of biblical prophecy and the establishment of God's kingdom on earth, and our blindness was necessary for a time for all other to be unblinded, but we are now coming to an active role in bringing about God's plan for the world.

In conclusion, let your heart not be troubled for the end of this age. Though many question the plan of God, His judgement is absolute. This book is just a primer or guide for anyone who wants to know more about His Biblical plan for the House of Isra'el and the people who agree to the message of Jesus. It is my hope that readers will find it informative and elevating in their understanding of the mysteries in the Bible; that by returning to the Hebrew language, the people of יְהֹוָה, and the land of God, we can become more complete ambassadors of God's kingdom and a more effective witnesses to the world around us. May the Lord

The Testament of Mikha'el

bless and keep you as you continue on your journey of faith and may you find joy and fulfillment in following His ways.

Torah Passages

Matthew 5:17-20 - "Do not think that I have come to abolish the Law or the Prophets; I have not come to abolish them but to fulfill them. For truly, I say to you, until heaven and earth pass away, not an iota, not a dot, will pass from the Law until all is accomplished. Therefore, whoever relaxes one of the least of these commandments and teaches others to do the same will be called least in the kingdom of heaven, but whoever does them and teaches them will be called great in the kingdom of heaven. For I tell you, unless your righteousness exceeds that of the scribes and Pharisees, you will never enter the kingdom of heaven."

John 14:15 - "If you love me, you will keep my commandments."

Deuteronomy 6:4-9: "Hear, O Israel: The Lord our God, the Lord is one. Love the Lord your God with all your heart and with all your soul and with all your strength. These commandments that I give you today are to be on your hearts. Impress them on your children. Talk about them when you sit at home and when you walk along the road, when you lie down and when you get up. Tie them as symbols on your hands and bind them on your foreheads. Write them on the doorframes of your houses and on your gates."

The Testament of Mikha'el

This passage emphasizes the importance of loving God and keeping His commandments. It instructs us to teach our children to do the same and to make God's commandments a part of every aspect of our lives.

Leviticus 19:18: "Do not seek revenge or bear a grudge against anyone among your people but love your neighbor as yourself. I am the Lord."

This passage teaches us to treat others with love and respect, and to avoid revenge or grudges. It emphasizes the importance of treating all people in the manner you prefer to be treated.

Isaiah 58:13-14 - "If thou turn away thy foot from the Sabbath, from doing thy pleasure on my holy day; and call the Sabbath a delight, the holy of the Lord, honourable; and shalt honour him, not doing thine own ways, nor finding thine own pleasure, nor speaking thine own words: Then shalt thou delight thyself in the Lord; and I will cause thee to ride upon the high places of the earth, and feed thee with the heritage of Jacob thy father: for the mouth of the Lord hath spoken it."

Exodus 20:8-11: "Remember the Sabbath day by keeping it holy. Six days you shall labor and do all your work, but the seventh day is a sabbath to the Lord your God. On it you shall not do any work, neither you, nor your son or daughter, nor your male or female servant, nor your animals, nor any foreigner residing in your towns. For in six days the Lord made the heavens and the earth, the sea, and all that is in them, but he rested on the seventh day. Therefore, the Lord blessed the Sabbath day and made it holy." This passage teaches us to do the Sabbath day as a day of rest and worship. It emphasizes the importance of taking time to rest and reflect on God's goodness and provision.

Deuteronomy 16:16-17: "Three times a year all your men must appear before the Lord your God at the place he will choose: at the Festival of Unleavened Bread, the Festival of Weeks and the Festival of Tabernacles. No one should appear before the Lord empty-handed. Each of you must bring a gift in proportion to the way the Lord your God has blessed you."

This passage teaches us to observe the Appointed Feast Days and to bring offerings in proportion to the way God has blessed us. It emphasizes the importance of celebrating and remembering God's goodness and provision.

Deuteronomy 24:14-15: "Do not take advantage of a hired worker who is poor and needy, whether that worker is a fellow Israelite or a foreigner residing in one of your towns. Pay them their wages each day before sunset, because they are poor and are counting on it. Otherwise, they may cry to the Lord against you, and you will be guilty of sin."

The Testament of Mikha'el

This passage teaches us to treat workers with fairness and to pay them promptly for their labor. It emphasizes the importance of showing compassion and justice to those who are in need.

John 3:16 "For God so loved the world that He gave His only begotten Son, that whoever believes in Him should not perish but have everlasting life. For God did not send His Son into the world to condemn the world, but that the world through Him might be saved."

Luke 16:17 "But it is easier for the heaven and earth to pass away than for one stroke of a letter in the Torah to become void."

Matthew 5:17 (NIV) "Do not think that I have come to abolish the Law or the Prophets; I have not come to abolish them but to fulfill them."

Hebrews 4:12,13 "For the word of God is alive and active. Sharper than any double-edged sword, it penetrates even to dividing soul and spirit, joints and marrow; it judges the thoughts and attitudes of the heart. Nothing in all creation is hidden from God's sight. Everything is uncovered and laid bare before the eyes of him to whom we must give account."

Works Cited

Voice of Prophecy. "Who Was Barabbas in the Bible?" *Bibleinfo.com*, Voice of Prophecy, https://www.bibleinfo.com/en/questions/barabbas.

Blackmon, Douglas A. *Slavery by Another Name: The Re-Enslavement of Black Americans from the Civil War to World War II*. Anchor Books, a Division of Random House, Inc., 2009.

Arnwine, Hannah G. *Prophesy from Arnwine Family*, "Yahowah said tell your dad I love him, I hear him, and it's about to end. Jerusalem has got to come down and its coming down today.", 23 Apr. 2023

Himmelstein, Kathryn E. W., et al. "*Association Between Racial Wealth Inequities and Racial Disparities in Longevity Among US Adults and Role of Reparations Payments, 1992 to 2018.*" JAMA Network Open, vol. 5, no. 11, American Medical Association, Nov. 2022, p. e2240519. https://doi.org/10.1001/jamanetworkopen.2022.40519.

Keys', A. (2004, October 26). "Marriage can't be understood apart from procreation". *Illinois Senate Debate*. Illinois.

The Testament of Mikha'el

Retrieved January 1, 2023, from
https://www.ontheissues.org/domestic/Alan_Keyes_Civil_Rights.htm

About the Author

Michael's parents, Michael W. Arnwine and Ramona, introduced him to the Lord of the Bible when he was a youngster, and ever since Michael's early years, he has had a profound connection to faith and the growth of his spirituality. Michael W. Arnwine and Ramona. Their goal was for him to achieve a profound comprehension of the love that Christ has for his followers and to acquire a divine perspective on life.

Michael came into contact with Rabbi Ralph Messer, a controversial and radical rabbi, while he was serving in the military and later while he was in a senior position in a church. Michael and his wife spent about three and a half years attending Yeshiva classes while Rabbi Messer directed their education. They investigated the possibility, based on Rabbi Messer's teachings, that ancient Israelites may have descended from indigenous Americans and Africans who had been enslaved at various points in American history. This viewpoint was reinforced by a number of scriptural references, including Deuteronomy 28 as well as Psalms 129 and Amos 9:7. This spiritual journey, which lasted for almost a decade, served as a transformative wilderness experience for them. It shaped their character and taught them to trust in the unfolding plan that God has for them, and it taught them to yield to His guidance and wisdom.

Michael accepted the role of a pastoral leader and accepted the responsibility of guiding and leading a community along the road of Torah as the transformative period that had been occurring was drawing to a close. It was during this time that he crossed paths with JediYah Melek and his family. JediYah Melek's family had a talent of teaching ancient biblical Hebrew, which contributed to forming the essential training for correctly interpreting the Word of God and accepting the calling of being a leader in Israel. JediYah Melek's gift helped him embrace the called of becoming a leader in Israel.

Visit hebrewisraelitescriptures.com, where more information and resources pertaining to the Hebrew language and the Hebrew Israelite scriptures may be found, if you are interested in delving further into studying the Hebrew language and investigating the Hebrew Israelite scriptures.

www.ingramcontent.com/pod-product-compliance
Lightning Source LLC
Chambersburg PA
CBHW042054060526
44107CB00157B/1280/J